science for a changing world

Prepared in cooperation with the Louisiana State University Agricultural Center

Baseline Data for Evaluating the Development Trajectory and Provision of Ecosystem Services by Created Fringing Oyster Reefs in Vermilion Bay, Louisiana

By Megan K. La Peyre, Lindsay Schwarting, and Shea Miller

Open-File Report 2013–1053

U.S. Department of the Interior
U.S. Geological Survey

U.S. Department of the Interior
KEN SALAZAR, Secretary

U.S. Geological Survey
Suzette M. Kimball, Acting Director

U.S. Geological Survey, Reston, Virginia: 2013

This and other USGS information products are available at http://store.usgs.gov/
U.S. Geological Survey
Box 25286, Denver Federal Center
Denver, CO 80225

To learn about the USGS and its information products visit http://www.usgs.gov/
1-888-ASK-USGS

Suggested citation:
La Peyre, M.K., Schwarting, Lindsay, and Miller, Shea, 2013, Baseline data for evaluating development trajectory and provision of ecosystem services of created fringing oyster reefs in Vermilion Bay, Louisiana: U.S. Geological Survey Open-File Report 2013–1053, 43 p.

Acknowledgments

We thank the many people who were critical in completing field work, processing samples in the lab, and providing boats and boat support including Louisiana State University Agricultural Center students and employees: Gary Decossas, Bran Wagner, Phil Westbrook, Aaron Honig, Austin Humphries, Steve Beck, Ben Eberline, Molly Rybovich, Jessica Furlong, Laura Brown, Mark Miller, Brandon Edwards, Cheryl Duplechain, Sandra Casas, Jerome La Peyre, Jon Risinger, Steve Hall; Louisiana Department of Wildlife and Fisheries employees: Paul Cook, Heather Finley; Oratech: Tyler Ortego; and The Nature Conservancy staff: Cindy Brown, Amy Smith-Kyle, Seth Blitch, Bryan Piazza, and Richard Martin. We thank Darrel Anders (USGS-NWRC) for boat support. Thanks to Dr. Stephen Scyphers and Dr. Lesley Baggett for comments that improved this report. This study was performed under the auspices of Louisiana State University IACUC protocols #08-005 and 11-006. Funding for this work was through a contract from The Nature Conservancy of Louisiana to Louisiana State University Agricultural Center.

Contents

Figures

Tables

Conversion Factors

Multiply	By	To obtain
Length		
centimeter (cm)	0.3937	inch (in.)
millimeter (mm)	0.03937	inch (in.)
meter (m)	3.281	foot (ft)
meter (m)	1.094	yard (yd)
Area		
square meter (m^2)	0.0002471	acre
square meter (m^2)	10.76	square foot (ft^2)
Volume		
liter (L)	33.82	ounce, fluid (fl. oz)
liter (L)	2.113	pint (pt)
liter (L)	1.057	quart (qt)
liter (L)	0.2642	gallon (gal)
cubic centimeter (cm^3)	0.06102	cubic inch (in^3)
liter (L)	61.02	cubic inch (in^3)
Mass		
gram (g)	0.03527	ounce, avoirdupois (oz)

Inch/Pound to SI

Multiply	By	To obtain
Length		
foot (ft)	0.3048	meter (m)

Temperature in degrees Celsius (°C) may be converted to degrees Fahrenheit (°F) as follows:
°F=(1.8×°C)+32

Vertical coordinate information is referenced to the North American Vertical Datum of 1988 (NAVD 88).

Concentrations of chemical constituents in water are given either in milligrams per liter (mg/L) or in micrograms per liter (µg/L).

Baseline Data for Evaluating the Development Trajectory and Provision of Ecosystem Services by Created Fringing Oyster Reefs in Vermilion Bay, Louisiana

By Megan K. La Peyre,[1] Lindsay Schwarting,[2] and Shea Miller[2]

Abstract

Understanding the time frame in which ecosystem services (that is, water quality maintenance, shoreline protection, habitat provision) are expected to be provided is important when restoration projects are being designed and implemented. Restoration of three-dimensional shell habitats in coastal Louisiana and elsewhere presents a valuable and potentially self-sustaining approach to providing shoreline protection, enhancing nekton habitat, and providing water quality maintenance. As with most restoration projects, the development of expected different ecosystem services often occurs over varying time frames, with some services provided immediately and others taking longer to develop.

This project was designed initially to compare the provision and development of ecosystem services by created fringing shoreline reefs in subtidal and intertidal environments in Vermilion Bay, Louisiana. Specifically, the goal was to test the null hypothesis that over time, the oyster recruitment and development of a sustainable oyster reef community would be similar at both intertidal and subtidal reef bases, and these sustainable reefs would in time provide similar shoreline stabilization, nekton habitat, and water quality services over similar time frames. Because the ecosystem services hypothesized to be provided by oyster reefs reflect long-term processes, fully testing the above-stated null hypothesis requires a longer-time frame than this project allowed. As such, this project was designed to provide the initial data on reef development and provision of ecosystem services, to identify services that may develop immediately, and to provide baseline data to allow for longer-term follow up studies tracking reef development over time.

Unfortunately, these initially created reef bases (subtidal, intertidal) were not constructed as planned because of the Deepwater Horizon oil spill in April 2010, which resulted in reef duplicates being created 6 months apart. Further confounding the project were additional construction and restoration projects along the same shorelines which occurred between 2011 and June 2012. Because of constant activity near and around the reefs and continuing construction, development trajectories could not be compared among reef types at this time. This report presents the data collected at the sites over 3 years (2010-2012), describing only conditions and trends. In addition, these data provide an extensive and detailed dataset

[1]U.S. Geological Survey, Louisiana Cooperative Fish and Wildlife Research Unit, School of Renewable Natural Resources, Louisiana State University Agricultural Center, Baton Rouge, LA 70803.
[2]School of Renewable Natural Resources, Louisiana State University Agricultural Center, Baton Rouge, LA 70803.

documenting initial conditions and initial ecosystem changes which will prove valuable in future data collection and analyses of reef development at this site.

Data collection characterized the local water quality conditions (salinity, temperature, total suspended sediments, dissolved oxygen, chlorophyll *a*), adjacent marsh vegetation, soils, and shoreline position along the project shoreline at Vermilion Bay. During the study, marsh vegetation and soil characteristics were similar across the study area and did not change over time. Shoreline movement indicated shoreline loss at all sites, which varied by reefs. Water quality conditions followed expected seasonal patterns for this region, and no significant nonseasonal changes were measured throughout the study period. Despite oyster recruitment in fall 2010 and 2011, few if any oysters survived from the 2010 year class to 2012. At the last sampling of this project, some oysters recruited in fall 2011 survived through 2012, resulting in an on-reef density of 18.3 ± 2.1 individuals per square meter (mean size: 85.6 ± 2.2 millimeters). Because project goals were to compare reef development and provision of ecosystem services over time, as well as many of the processes identified for monitoring reflect long-term processes, results and data are presented only qualitatively, and trends or observations should be interpreted cautiously at this point. Measurable system responses to reef establishment require more time than was available for this study. These data provide a valuable baseline that can be ultimately used to help inform site selections for future restoration projects as well to further investigate the development trajectories of ecosystem provision of created reefs in this region.

Introduction

Restoration of three-dimensional shell habitats in coastal Louisiana presents a valuable and potentially self-sustaining approach to providing shoreline protection, enhancing nekton habitat, and maintaining water quality (Coen and others, 1999, 2007; Peterson and others, 2003; Scyphers and others, 2011). As with most restoration projects, the development of expected, different ecosystem services (that is, water quality maintenance, shoreline protection, habitat provision) often occurs over varying time frames with some services provided immediately, whereas others may take as long as two decades to develop (that is, Odum, 1969; Craft and others, 1999; La Peyre and others, 2008). In order to accurately account for service provision and to properly evaluate the success of a restoration project, full understanding of the time-frame in which ecosystem services are expected to function is important. The development and ecological trajectory of restored ecosystems has long been investigated and borrows heavily from studies on ecological succession, community ecology, and ecosystem development (Odum, 1969). Although numerous studies have documented marsh restoration development trajectories, few studies that we are aware of have addressed the development trajectories of functional oyster reefs within coastal waters.

This project was designed initially to compare the provision and development of ecosystem services over time between created subtidal and intertidal oyster reefs. Specifically, the goal was to test the null hypothesis that over time, the recruitment and development of a sustainable oyster reef community would be similar at both intertidal and subtidal reef bases, and these sustainable reefs would in time provide similar shoreline stabilization, nekton habitat, and water quality services. Because the ecosystem services hypothesized to be provided by oyster reefs reflect long-term processes, fully testing the above-stated null hypothesis requires a longer-time frame than this project allowed. As such, this project was designed to provide the initial data on reef development, as well as provision of ecosystem services, to allow for longer-term follow-up studies tracking reef development over time.

The Nature Conservancy, working with local landowners (Audubon Society) and construction and engineering companies, developed and implemented the artificial reef creation. From 2010 through 2012, we collected preconstruction and postconstruction physiochemical and biological data to quantify changes in reefs and to identify their provision of ecosystem services over time. Although the initial project design called for comparison of subtidal and intertidal reefs with reference sites, all duplicated along the same shoreline, many factors contributed to continued project changes. The Deepwater Horizon oil spill, along with the restoration community's desire to continue to implement further artificial reef segments, resulted in the addition of four subtidal reef segments and two reference sites along the shoreline of Southwest Pass, La., immediately east of the Vermilion Cove shoreline, and the addition of duplicate, new intertidal (intertidal gap) and new subtidal (subtidal 2) shoreline segments along Vermilion Cove. This rolling construction activity resulted in mismatched sample dates, uneven reef ages, and an inability to follow a controlled experimental design. As a result, this report provides an overview and description of reef and shoreline specific soil, marsh, and water quality characteristics, shoreline movement, oyster recruitment and survival, and nekton use associated with each reef segment over the last 3 years.

Presented herein are the data collected between January 2010 and October 2012, which include preconstruction data, and postconstruction monitoring, with installation dates for different units ranging from April 2010 to June 2012. These data provide a detailed overview of reef recruitment, marsh status, shoreline movement, and nekton abundances within the experimental area. Because 5 years of postconstruction data are generally recommended to fully assess the effectiveness of reef restoration (*http://www.oyster-restoration.org/scsg04/ SCSG04.pdf*; accessed February 1, 2013), these data present only a very short-term view of the impact of the projects (from 6 to 20 months [mo] after construction).

Study Area

This project was located in Vermilion Bay, La., in two locations adjacent to land owned by the Audubon Society (Rainey Refuge) (fig. 1). One location is situated facing south (Vermilion Cove) in protected, shallow waters (fig. 2). The Vermilion Cove shoreline is composed of silt/clay and oyster shell fragments. The area in front of the shore has a low depth profile with the entire bay averaging less than 1 (m) water depth under mean water conditions. Shoreline profiles range from receding beach/vegetation fronts to shallow cut-bank edges (20-40 centimeters [cm]). The other location (Southwest Pass) is located on a northeast-facing shore along a busy navigation channel with comparatively swift water and a large fetch (fig. 3). Southwest Pass sites have a relatively steep edge and are exposed constantly to large workboat wakes and wind-generated waves. Both sites are located adjacent to one of Louisiana's public oyster seed grounds although the area has not been highly productive for oyster harvest in recent years because of increased input of freshwater from the Atchafalaya River, which results in low salinity during the summer months in many years (*http://www.wlf.louisiana.gov/sites/default/files/pdf/page_fishing/32695-Oyster%20Program/2011_oyster_stock_assessment.pdf*; accessed February 1, 2013).

Figure 1.   Map of study area located in Vermilion Bay, Louisiana. The oyster reefs were placed adjacent to shorelines in Southwest Pass and Vermilion Cove.

4

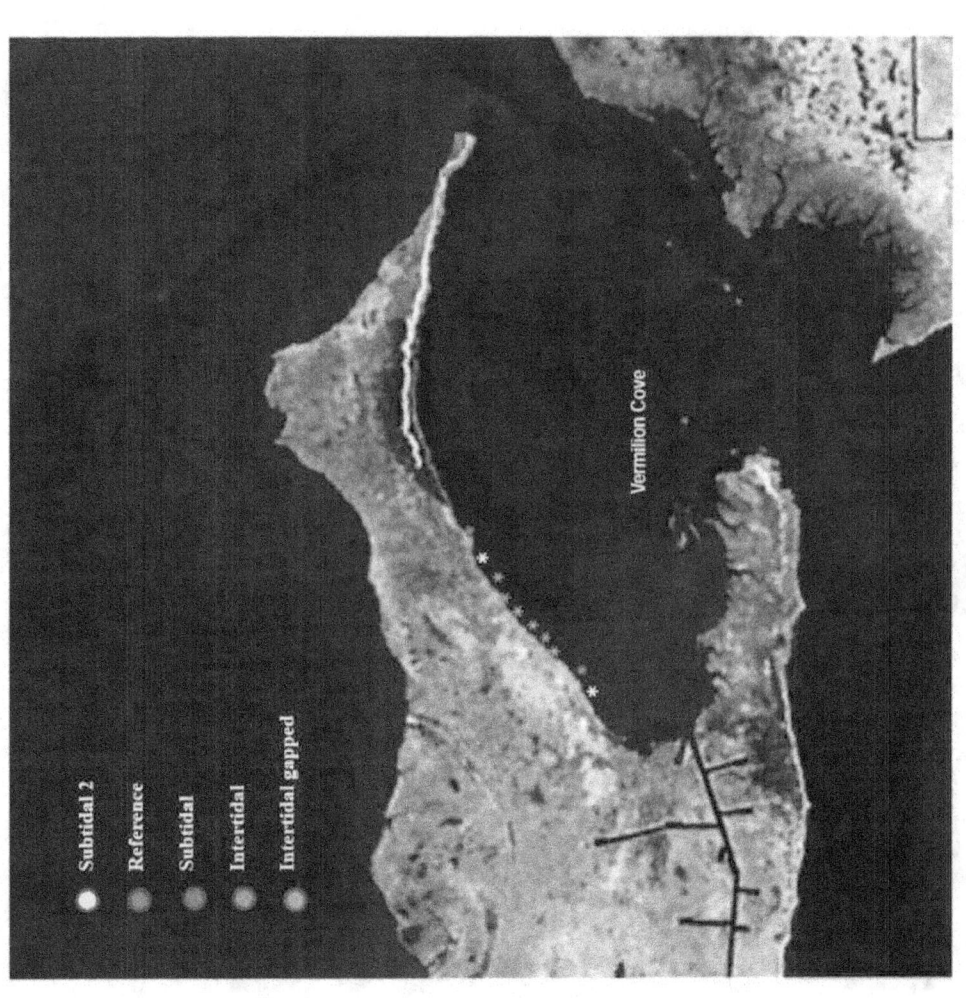

Figure 2. Location of 10 study sites (8 reef and 2 reference) along the shoreline by Vermilion Cove, Louisiana. Each reef constructed was 68.5 meters (m) long and a minimum of 75 m apart.

5

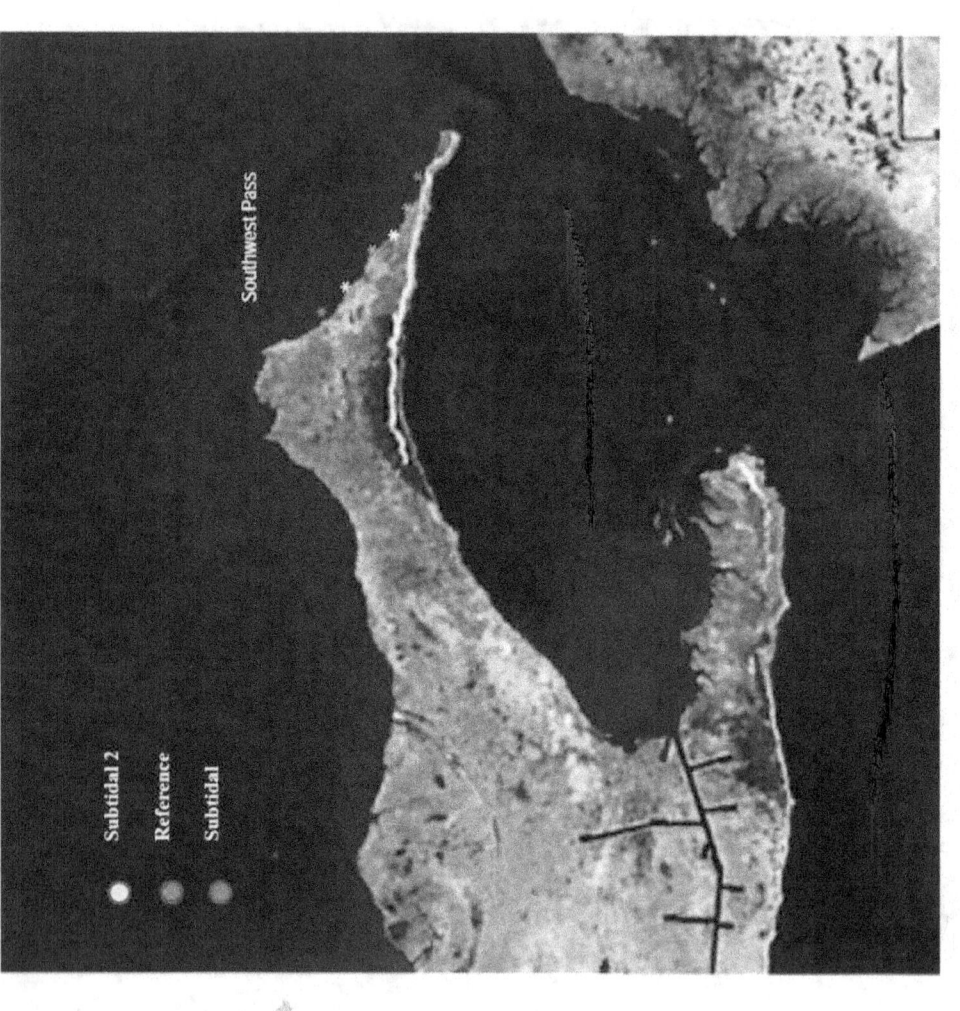

Figure 3.   Location of 6 study sites (4 reef and 2 reference) within Southwest Pass, Louisiana. Reefs are 68.5-meters (m) long with a minimum of 75 m between each reef.

Reef Construction and Sampling Schedule

Originally established as a controlled, duplicated designed experiment, because of funding opportunities available to the restoration community for specific projects along the exact same shoreline of this project, the project evolved significantly with continued restoration and creation activities along the project shorelines (table 1). The continual activities within the project area between March 2010 and June 2012, along with mismatched construction caused by the Deepwater Horizon oil spill, resulted in our inability to statistically compare sites or to draw any conclusions; we do, however, present a valuable baseline dataset for all of the activities that occurred within our study area.

Table 1. General timeline of preconstruction, construction, and postconstruction activities for research sites in Vermilion Cove and Southwest Pass, Louisiana. Multiple sample events occurred in SPR2011, SUM2011, and SPR2012. Reference sites at Vermilion Cove are not divided into preconstruction and postconstruction because of the wide range of construction dates and the loss of the original sampled reference sites because of placement of reefs on the reference site.

[SPR, March–May; SUM, June–August; FAL, September–November; WIN, December–February]

	SPR2010	SUM2010	FAL2010	WIN2010	SPR2011	SUM2011	FAL2011	WIN2011	SPR2012	SUM2012	FAL2012
Vermilion Cove											
Subtidal (T1)											
Preconstruction	X										
Construction	REP A		REP B								
Postconstruction						X	X		X	X	X
Intertidal (T2)											
Preconstruction	X										
Construction	REP A		REP B								
Postconstruction						X	X		X	X	X
Intertidal-gap (T3)											
Preconstruction	X										
Construction						REP A/B X					
Postconstruction							X		X	X	X
Subtidal 2 (T4)											
Preconstruction											
Construction						X			REP A/B		
Postconstruction										X	X
Reference (REF)											
Preconstruction											
Construction											
Postconstruction						X	X		X	X	X
Sampling	X		X		X	X	X		X	X	X

8

Table 1. General timeline of preconstruction, construction, and postconstruction activities for research sites in Vermilion Cove and Southwest Pass, Louisiana. Multiple sample events occurred in SPR2011, SUM2011, and SPR2012. Reference sites at Vermilion Cove are not divided into preconstruction and postconstruction because of the wide range of construction dates and the loss of the original sampled reference sites because of placement of reefs on the reference site.—Continued

[SPR, March-May; SUM, June-August; FAL, September-November; WIN, December-February]

	Southwest Pass	
	Subtidal (T1)	
Presconstruction	X	
Construction		REP A/B
Postconstruction		X
	Subtidal 2 (T4)	
Presconstruction	X	
Construction		REP A/B
Postconstruction		X
	Reference (REF)	
Sampling	X	X

This project was initiated in Vermilion Cove with three treatments, each duplicated. Two reference shoreline segments, two created subtidal reef segments, and two created intertidal reef segments were identified with a minimum of 75 m between each segment. The Nature Conservancy contracted with a local consulting company to create reefs by using either a single layer (subtidal), or a double layer (intertidal) of Oysterbreak^{TM} rings (fig. 4). In April 2010, the first duplicate of each reef treatment (hereinafter subtidal Rep A; intertidal Rep A) was constructed. Further reef placement was stopped because of the Deepwater Horizon oil spill, and access to sites was highly restricted. In October 2010, construction of the second replicate of each treatment was completed (hereinafter subtidal Rep B; intertidal Rep B). This 6-mo difference in reef creation dates prevented us from examining reef development trajectories by using the designed replicates as originally planned.

Figure 4.   Layout of artificial reef bases and reef design. *A*, View of subtidal artificial reef substrate bases during very low water; reefs consist of a double wide, single height layer of rings placed 30 meters off the shoreline. Subtidal rings are 50.8 centimeters (cm) tall, whereas subtidal 2 rings are 61.0 cm tall. *B*, View of intertidal artificial reef substrate bases; intertidal substrates consist of a double ring layer on the bottom, topped by a single ring layer. Intertidal design is continuous; intertidal gapped (shown) is missing every fifth and sixth top ring.

11

Further project changes came during 2011 and 2012 with additional construction of artificial reefs along the same shoreline. In June 2011, duplicate intertidal gapped reefs were created. Intertidal- gap consisted of a double layer of Oysterbreak^{TM} rings, with the fifth and sixth top ring missing to create gaps for fish passage. This new set of reefs was placed on the original reference sites, and we established new reference sites outside the construction area. In June 2011, the original subtidal and intertidal reefs were lengthened so that all six constructed reef treatments were of equal length (68.5 m). Again, these changes resulted in impacts to our study sites because of construction activities and in substitution of our original reference sites.

In March 2012, two more segments of the subtidal reef of similar length were constructed at Southwest Pass; in June 2012, duplicate reef segments of subtidal 2 reef (similar to original subtidal reef but 10 cm taller) were built in Vermilion Cove and Southwest Pass, resulting in an addition of six new reef segments and associated reference sites at Southwest Pass. A timeline of preconstruction and postconstruction sampling is outlined in tables 1 and 2. All sites had three randomly identified sample points along the reef length where sampling occurred.

Table 2. Schedule of actual sampling activities for reef and reference sites at Southwest Pass and Vermilion Cove in Vermilion Bay, Louisiana.

	SPR2010	SUM2010	FAL2010	WIN2010	SPR2011	SUM2011	FAL2011	WIN2011	SPR2012	SUM2012	FAL2012
Shoreline		X			X	X			X	X	
Survey							X				X
Vegetation	X	X	X		X	X			X	X	
Soils	X	X	X		X	X			X	X	
Water quality	X	X	X		X	X	X		X	X	
Nekton (transient)	X	X				X	X		X	X	
Nekton (resident)						X				X	
Oysters	X	X	X	X	X	X	X	X	X	X	X
Recruitment							X				X

13

Project Methods

Shoreline Stabilization and Adjacent Marsh Vigor

Shoreline stabilization was measured following Meyer and others (1997) and Piazza and others (2005). At each sample point (three along each experimental reef or reference), five permanent base stakes were located in the marsh. A tape measure was used to determine the distance from the base stake to the shoreline edge. Shoreline edge is defined as the farthest waterward extent of the wetland macrophytes. To ensure consistent measurements, shoreline edge was measured along a set compass heading.

To measure change in soil volume and shoreline slope change, a reference (Vermilion Cove) and one intertidal reef site (intertidal Rep A) were selected for detailed transect surveys by using a TOPCON GTS-226 electronic total station. Preconstruction (reef: November 2010; reference: February 2011) and postconstruction (both Nov 2012) transects (five, 35 m) running from on the marsh perpendicular into the water were completed, recording elevation every 1 m along set compass points and resulting in more than 60 point measurements. Different preconstruction dates for reference are due to the movement of our reference site. Changes in shoreline slope and soil volume located behind the reef were calculated by using the Surfer 8.03 Surface Mapping System. Surfaces created from separate samplings were overlaid, and a change in sediment volume (cm^3 mo^{-1}) based on elevations was calculated through Surfer.

Aboveground and belowground vegetation density and biomass, and soil percent organic matter and bulk density were quantified in triplicate at each sample point. At each sample point, triplicate quarter meter quadrats were haphazardly thrown to land within 1 m of the shoreline edge. Percentage of vegetative cover by species was recorded. All aboveground biomass was removed, returned to the lab at the Louisiana State University (LSU) AgCenter and quantified in the laboratory by drying to a constant biomass (gram [g]), and recording biomass by species. Within each quadrat, duplicate 5 x 15 cm cores were collected. One core was used to quantify belowground vegetative biomass by rinsing all sediment through a 3-mm sieve, and drying vegetative material to a constant biomass (g). The second core was used to determine percentage of soil organic matter by using loss on ignition in a muffle furnace. Bulk density was also calculated from these cores prior to firing in the muffle furnace. Bulk density is calculated as grams per cubic centimeter.

Reef Sustainability

To better understand the dynamics of reef sustainability, oyster growth, mortality, condition, and *Perkinsus marinus* (Dermo) infection intensities were measured in experimental bags placed adjacent to the reefs. In 2011, two bags of 100 2.5-cm oysters spawned at the LSU Sea Grant Oyster Hatchery were placed adjacent to the reef. In 2012, five bags of 100 2.5-cm oysters spawned at the LSU Sea Grant Oyster Hatchery were placed adjacent to the reef. Size and mortality were measured bimonthly, and disease and condition of 15 oysters were measured bimonthly. Cumulative mortality was calculated for each year, and growth rates were calculated by using shell length ($GR = (SL_t - SL_{t-1})/(\# \text{ days}*30)$), where GR = growth rate; SL = shell length; and t = time). Growth rates were standardized to a 30-day month. These data are valuable in explaining on-reef observations of oyster population dynamics.

Because of difficulties encountered in sampling from the created reefs on submerged reefs in turbid waters, we established minireef prototypes, referred to as "reefsicles," at the Vermilion Cove site. These reefsicles consisted of small oysterkrete blocks epoxied to PVC poles and placed off-bottom (fig. 5). These reefsicles allowed us to track oyster recruitment and growth on the oysterkrete substrate by removing the reefsicles from the water to count and measure oysters. Nine reefsicles were placed behind the intertidal reef at Vermilion Cove in April 2011; of these 9 reefsicles, 3 were covered in predator exclusion cages in order to account for differences in oyster populations which may be attributed to predation mortality. Reefsicles were checked in October 2011 for recruitment and then removed completely in October 2012 for analysis. Any oyster recruitment was counted and measured. Because of the conclusion of reef construction in June 2012, and final sampling in August 2012 at Southwest Pass, no reefsicles were set out at this location.

October 2012

March 2011

Figure 5.   Reefsicles created and installed in Vermilion Cove for monitoring oyster recruitment. Clean oysterkrete material was epoxied to PVC poles, which were inserted in the sediment so that the oysterkrete block was off the bottom. Reefsicles were constructed in March 2011 and removed for analysis in October 2012.

Water Quality

Temperature (degrees Celsius [°C]), salinity, dissolved oxygen (milligrams per liter [mg L^{-1}]) were measured every field visit by using a YSI model 556 water quality meter (Yellow Springs Instruments, Ohio) at each sample point. Water clarity was measured by using a secchi disk (cm). Furthermore, two opaque bottles of water were collected at 0.5 m below the surface, and immediately adjacent to the reef, placed on ice, and taken back to the lab to be processed for total organic matter, total inorganic matter (mg L^{-1}), and chlorophyll a (micrograms per liter [μg L^{-1}]). Continuous data from the nearest continuous data recorder were downloaded, and discrete temperature and salinity values compared; hourly water-level data from the recorder were also used to calculate reef exposure times (LOCPR, 2012).

Habitat Enhancement

Nekton (fish and invertebrates) recruitment to and use of the constructed reef structures were assessed by using four gear types. Gill nets were used to capture the large, transient fish community. The 11-m experimental gill nets consisted of four panels, each 2.7 x 1.8 m and with mesh sizes 3.8, 5.1, 6.4, and 7.6 cm. The gill nets were placed perpendicular to the reefs, on the seaward side of the reefs, and soaked for 1 hour. All gill net samples were processed in the field by recording species identity, total length, and biomass. Time of day and water quality measurements were taken with each sample. Samples were taken during daylight hours.

To characterize the juvenile and resident nekton communities, five 2.4-meter (m) cast net samples were taken at each segment in the area between the reef and the marsh vegetation. Two 10-m seine pulls by using a 3-m bag seine (3-mm mesh) near the marsh edge and near the reef structure were collected. All cast net and seine samples were bagged, placed on ice, and returned to the lab for further processing which involved species identification and measurement of total length and weight by species.

Postconstruction resident communities at Vermilion Cove reefs were examined by deploying substrate trays filled with oyster shell in 2010, and again in 2011 and 2012. Trays were deployed at all sites in 2010 on the south side of the reefs, but we experienced a high loss of trays. In August 2011, trays were deployed adjacent to the reefs and at all reference sites and allowed to sit for 3 weeks before collection of all trays. This deployment was repeated in July 2012. Because of the impracticality of using nets to capture cryptic species that live within the complex oyster reef matrix, trays were used to characterize the smaller fish and invertebrate communities that are known to reside and frequent healthy reefs (Lehnert and Allen, 2002; Plunket and La Peyre, 2005; Yeager and Layman 2011). Each tray (0.22 m^2) was modified by attaching a drawstring bag net with fine mesh (2.6 mm^2). The sides of this net were gathered at the base of the tray while it was deployed, and prior to retrieval, the net was drawn tight to enclose the tray contents before bringing the tray to the surface, preventing the escape of more mobile organisms (Beck, 2011). All organisms were placed in sample bags and put on ice for transport to the laboratory at LSU where they were processed and species identification and total length and weight (g dry weight) were recorded. Density of organisms was calculated and the community described.

Analyses

Because of major differences in site environment and reef construction, Vermilion Cove and Southwest Pass are presented separately. For Vermilion Cove samples, because of continual construction from March 2010 through June 2012, data are presented and described qualitatively only. No direct comparisons are made because of the number of confounding factors making statistical comparisons, or direct comparisons with replicates, impossible.

Although sampling was of a very short time frame, Southwest Pass sediment and vegetation samples were analyzed, but treatments were constructed in March and June, and postconstruction samples are from June and July of the same year. By using a two-factor analysis of variance (ANOVA), we examined preconstruction and postconstruction and treatment differences (SAS; PROC GLIMMIX; factors: TIME: pre and post; TREATMENT: reference, subtidal, subtidal 2). When results were significant, a Tukey's test was used to identify significant differences. Aboveground and belowground vegetation biomass were log-transformed to achieve normality. Log-transformed nekton data (CPUE, richness) were analyzed by using a one-factor ANOVA (TREATMENT) with postconstruction data collected in summer 2012 only. Unless indicated otherwise, mean and standard errors are reported for all variables.

Results and Discussion

Vermilion Cove

Shoreline Stabilization

All sites experienced shoreline movement during the period of measurement, postconstruction, with the reference sites retreating a mean of 12.2 ± 7.6 cm mo^{-1}, and reef sites retreating an average of 6.5 ± 3.1 cm mo^{-1}. Within reef sites, there were differences in mean retreat with subtidal sites retreating 14.2 ± 3.6 cm mo^{-1} and the two intertidal treatments retreating an average of 4.1 ± 2.7 cm mo^{-1} (fig. 6). Survey results of just one reference (February 2011–November 2012) and one intertidal reef site (intertidal Rep A; Nov 2010–Nov 2012) show a larger decrease in soil volume at the reference site (0.18 cm^3 m^{-1} mo^{-1}) compared to the intertidal reef site (0.02 cm^3 m^{-1} mo^{-1}) (fig. 6). There was minimal change in slope at either site.

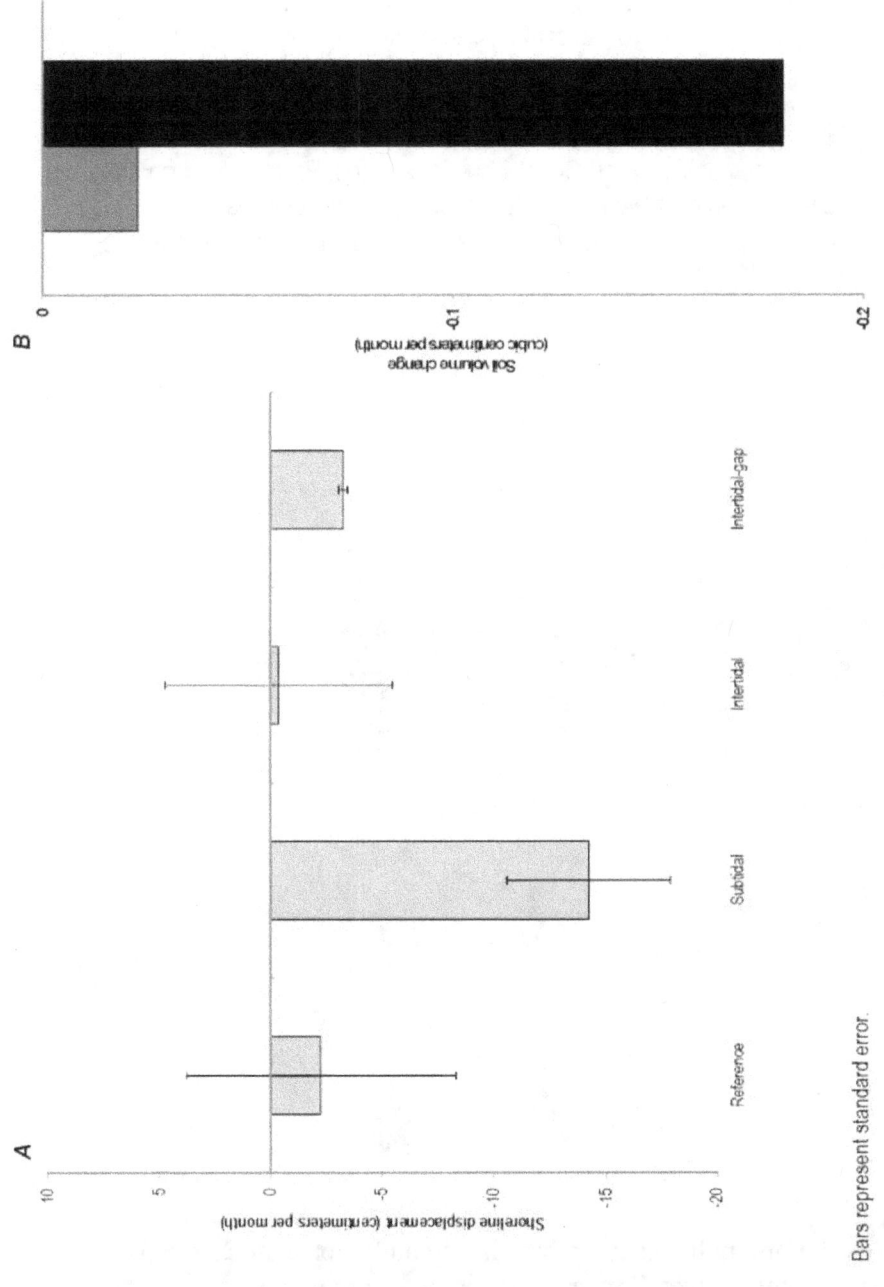

Bars represent standard error.

Figure 6.   Shoreline displacement and change in soil volume in Vermilion Bay, Louisiana. *A*, Shoreline displacement (centimeters per month [cm mo⁻¹]; 30-day month was used) for reference and reef treatments postconstruction (June 2011–July 2012). *B*, Change in soil volume between reef and shoreline based on differences in elevation and slopes shown in graphs. Only one treatment (gray) and one reference (black) site were surveyed.

19

Overall, mean percentage of vegetative cover across all Vermilion Cove sites was 38.3 percent (± 2.5). Dominant vegetative species at all sites was black needlerush (*Juncus roemerianus*) (27.3 ± 3.0 percent) and smooth cordgrass (*Spartina alterniflora*) (9.4 ± 1.5 percent). Other species detected at sites include *Distichlis spicata*, *Spartina patens*, *Phragmites australis*, and *Ipomoea sagittata*. Across all Vermilion Cove sites, aboveground vegetative biomass was 800.6 ± 54.0 g m^{-2} (fig. 7). Total belowground vegetative biomass was 295.2± 25.4 g m^{-2} (fig. 7).

Figure 7. Mean (standard error) aboveground and belowground vegetative biomass (grams per square meter [g m^{-2}]) of reference and treatments at Vermilion Cove, Louisiana, sites. Preconstruction samples for subtidal, intertidal, and intertidal-gap samples were collected in spring 2010, whereas preconstruction samples for subtidal 2 were collected in summer 2011. Reference represents all reference samples collected from fall 2010 through fall 2012.

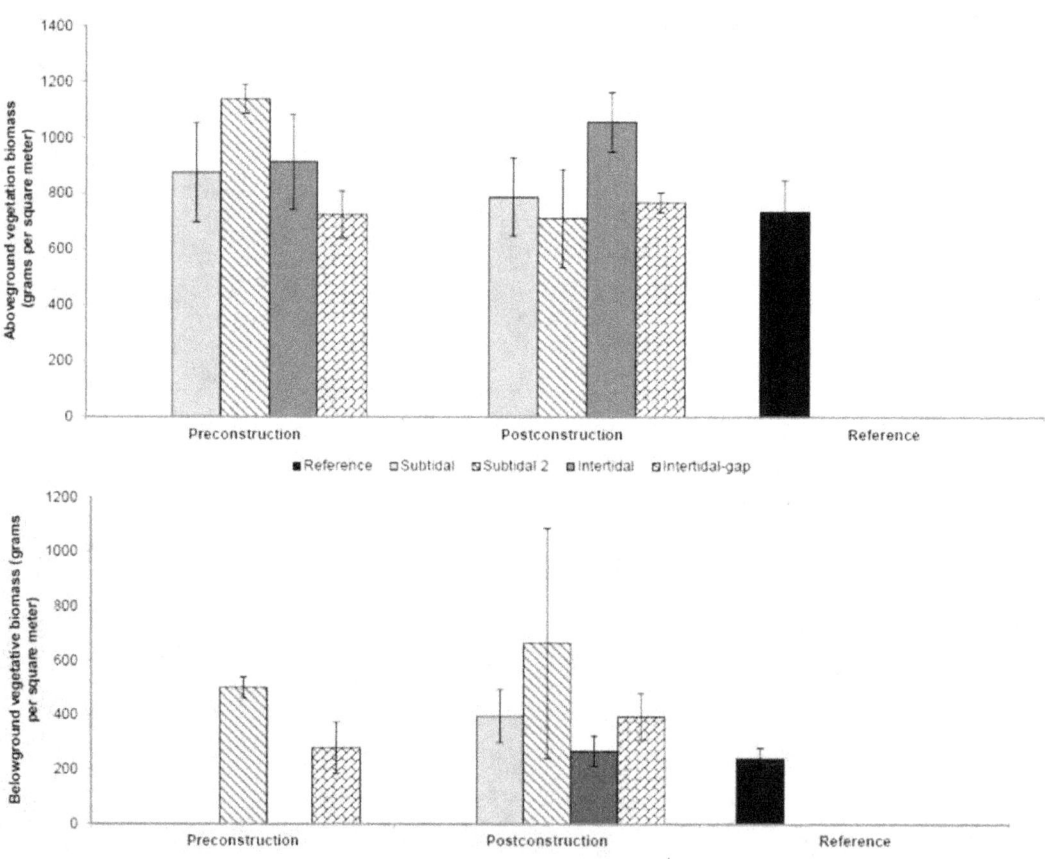

Percentage of organic matter and bulk density were significantly correlated, so only percentage of organic matter is presented. Overall mean percentage of organic matter across all Vermilion Cove sites was similar, averaging 3.6 ± 0.1 percent.

Reef Sustainability

Oyster growth cages indicated slow growth and relatively high mortality in both 2010 and 2011. In 2010, oysters experienced 71 percent mortality, with mean growth of remaining oysters at 3.0 mm mo^{-1} during spring 2010. No spat (young, immature oysters < 25 mm shell height) recruitment was detected until fall 2010, when all constructed reefs recruited spat with an estimated density of 300 individuals m^{-2}, and ranging in size from 10 to 50 mm in November 2010. Barnacles, algae, and mussels were evident on the reefs in the fall as well.

In 2011, cumulative oyster mortality was 89 percent, and mean growth for the year was 1.2 mm/mo (fig. 8). Despite the settlement noted in November 2010, no 1-year-old oysters were identified on the reefs in October 2011 indicating no survival. Reefsicles deployed in March 2011 were checked for recruitment in October 2011. Only five individuals with a mean size of 42.5 ± 10.5 mm were noted across nine reefsicle blocks; this size class suggests 2011 recruitment year class oysters only. Mortality from disease was not likely because infection of oysters by the parasite *Perkinsus marinus* was minimal (399.4 ± 165.0 spores g^{-1}) during 2011.

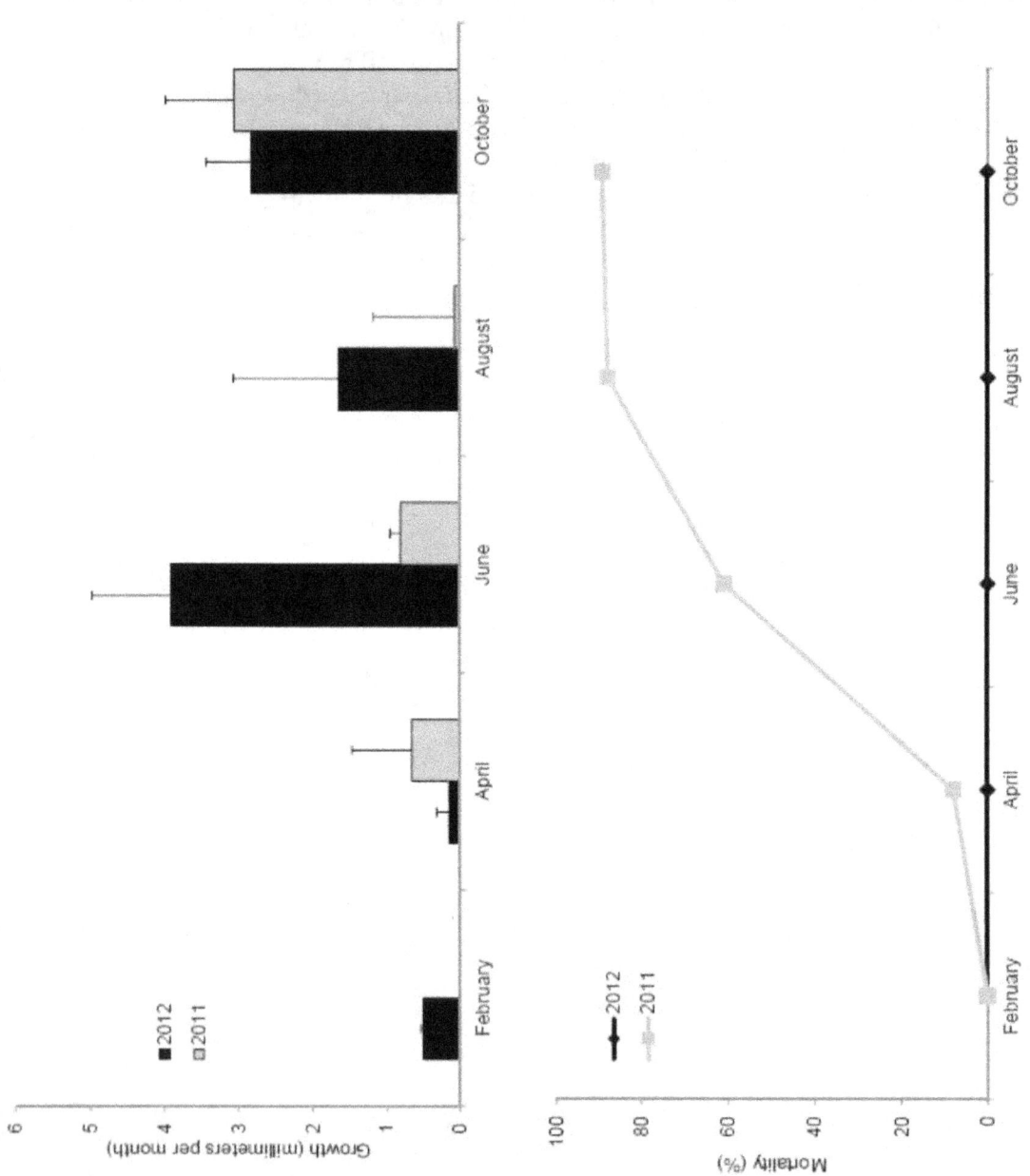

Figure 8.   Mean growth (± standard error) and cumulative mortality of oysters deployed in cages adjacent to Vermilion Cove, Louisiana, intertidal reef in 2011 and 2012.

22

In 2012, mean oyster growth was 1.8 mm mo^{-1} and cumulative mortality was 3 percent (fig. 8). The prevalence of infection by *P. marinus* in sampled oysters was moderate (53-80 percent); however, mean overall infection levels were extremely low (1,972.1 ± 1,790.9 spores g^{-1}).

Reefsicles placed adjacent to one of the intertidal reefs supported healthy recruitment of live oysters (fig. 5). All nine reefsicle blocks installed in March 2011 were recovered in October 2012 with visible recruitment. Predator-exclusion cages were not recovered and were likely lost because of weather or wave action. Overall, the reefsicles had a mean oyster density of 18.3 ± 2.1 individuals m^{-2}. Attached oysters were a mean size of 85.6 ± 2.2 mm in length indicating that in 2012, and possibly fall 2011, recruited oysters were surviving and growing.

Environmental Variables

Water quality parameters are reported as ranges across all dates and treatment types (table 3). At each site, temperature, dissolved oxygen, clarity, salinity, total particulate matter, and chlorophyll *a* varied as expected by season and year. Because of the proximity of sites, no differences were expected between sites or treatments, and data are presented as overall ranges and means. Salinity measurements were comparable to continuous data collected by Coastal Reference Monitoring System (CRMS0541; LOCPR, 2012) (fig. 9). Daily mean water levels collected by CRMS0541 from January 2010 to June 2012 were also used to characterize the different reef treatments with respect to water elevation (fig. 10). The top of the reef was at or above the water level or above at the intertidal reefs 89 percent of the time and at the intertidal-gap reefs for 84 percent of the time. For the subtidal 2 reefs, the top of the reef was at the water level or above for 22 percent of the time and at the subtidal reefs for 9 percent of the time.

Table 3. Range of water quality parameters measured at reef and reference sites at Vermilion Cove, Louisiana, across all dates and construction statuses. Southwest Pass, La., was only sampled in spring and summer months.

[Temp, temperature in degrees Celsius; DO, dissolved oxygen in milligrams per liter; Water clarity, secchi depth in centimeters; TSS, total suspended sediments in milligrams per liter; Chl. *a*, chlorophyll *a* in micrograms per liter]

	Vermilion Cove	Southwest Pass
Temp (°C)	14.6-33.5	24.3-30.9
DO (mg L^{-1})	0.3-9.2	5.2-7.8
Water clarity (cm)	6.0-67.0	17.0-62.0
Salinity	1.2-24.7	1.1-16.0
TSS (mg L^{-1})	5.3-593.3	29.3-195.3
Chl. *a* (µg L^{-1})	0.8-37.3	5.3-16.9

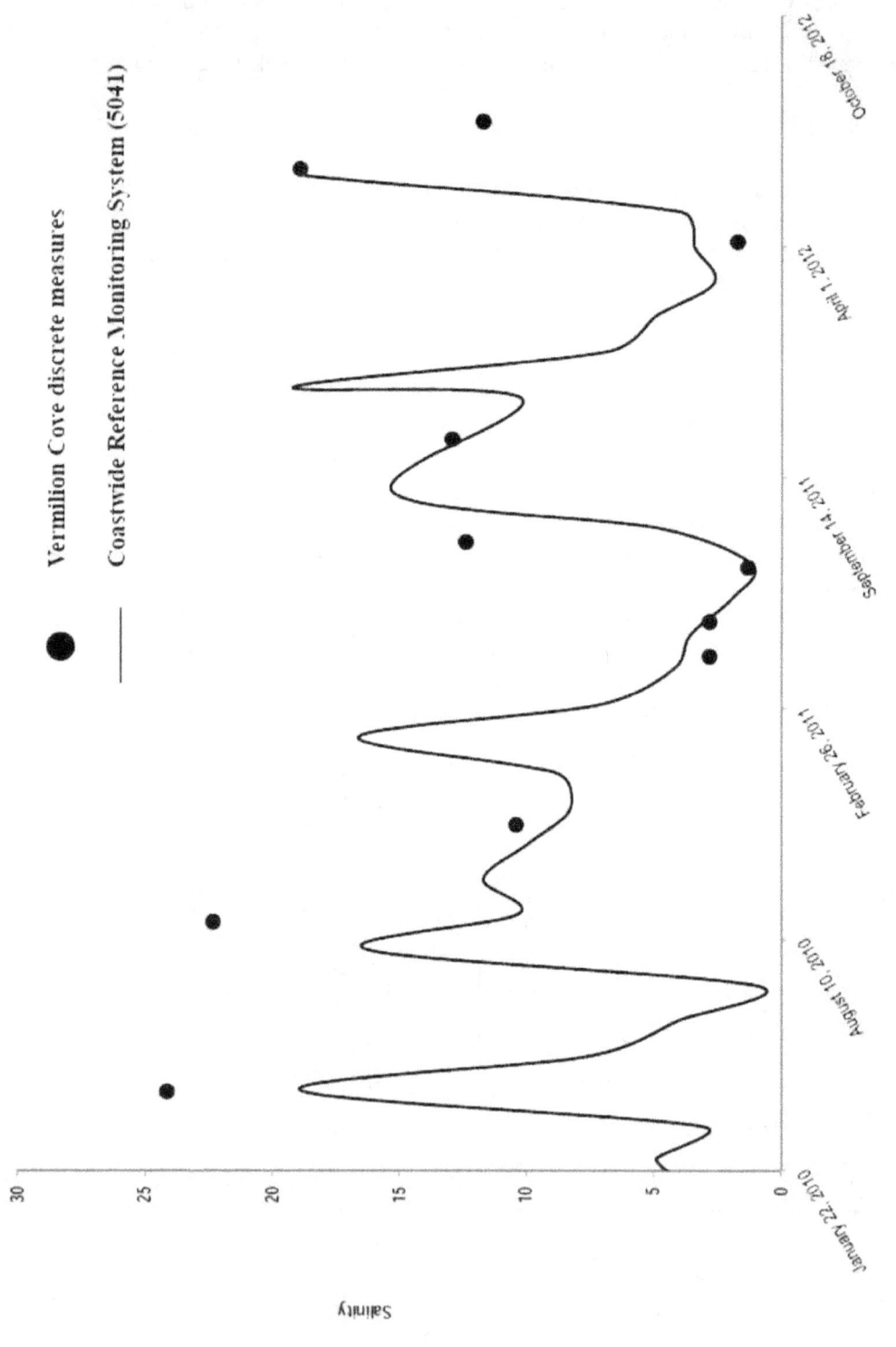

Figure 9.   Overall mean salinity of all study sites at Vermilion Cove and Southwest Pass, Louisiana, plotted with salinity data from the nearest continuous data recorder maintained by the State of Louisiana (CRMS 5041; LOCPR, 2012). Standard errors were all less than 0.3 and are not shown on the graph.

24

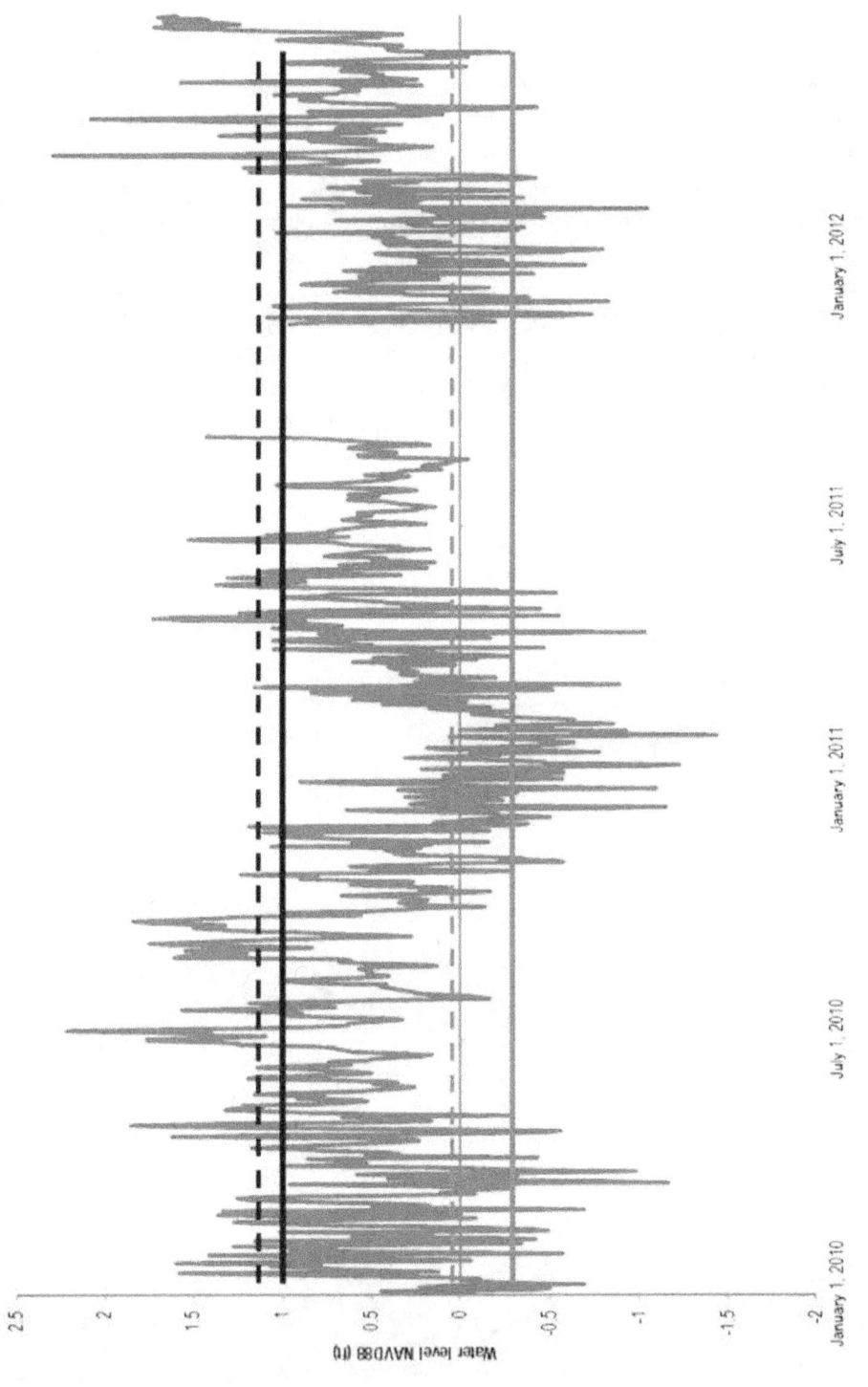

Lines in black represent the top elevations of the two intertidal sites (dashed = intertidal, solid = intertidal-gap. 84 percent of the time the reef top is above water). Lines in grey are the top elevations of the two subtidal sites (dashed = subtidal 2, 22 percent of the time the reef top is above water; solid = subtidal, 9 percent of the time the reef top is above water).

Figure 10. Daily mean water levels at Vermilion Cove, Louisiana (CRMS0541; LOCPR, 2012), from January 2010 to June 2012. Data are referenced to NAVD 88 (feet [ft]).

Habitat Enhancement

Because of unequal sample efforts, differences in construction dates spanning more than 2 years, and differences in timing of samples particularly for preconstruction samples, we present the nekton abundance and species richness data below and describe it qualitatively. Comparison of matching sample dates was considered, but because of the 2-year difference in reef age, and the continued construction in the vicinity, we felt that it was difficult to interpret any patterns that may emerge. Tables of species present only postconstruction samples for comparison.

A total of 60 gill net samples were collected over nine sampling periods in 2010 through 2012 in Vermilion Cove. In total, 163 individuals, consisting of 18 species of fish and invertebrates, were collected. CPUE ranged from 0.6 ± 0.6 to 4.5 ± 1.7 individuals per gill net hour fished, and species richness ranged from 0.3 ± 0.3 to 2.3 ± 0.6 (fig. 11). Because of differences in construction dates and in order to standardize species comparisons among treatments, table 4 includes just the postconstruction data for all reference and reef sites. In postconstruction samples, a total of 131 individuals were collected. The most abundant organisms were bull shark (*Carcharhinus leucas*) and hardhead catfish (*Ariopsis felis*), which composed 54 percent of the postconstruction samples.

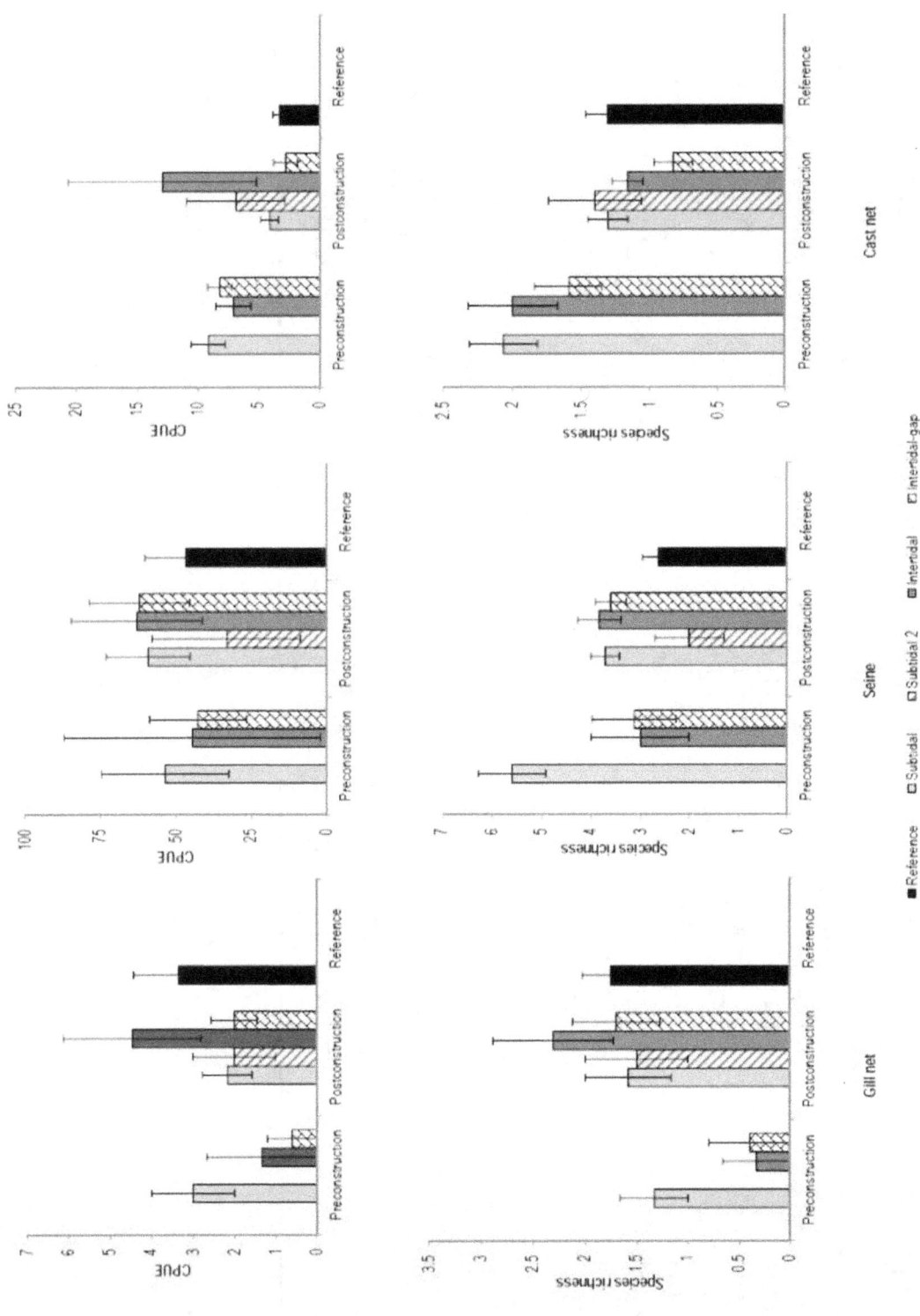

Figure 11.   Mean catch per unit effort (CPUE) and number of species caught with gill nets, seine, and cast nets at reference, subtidal, subtidal 2, intertidal, and intertidal-gap reefs at Vermilion Cove, Louisiana. Bars represent standard error. Preconstruction samples for subtidal, intertidal, and intertidal-gap samples were collected in spring 2010. Reference samples collected from fall 2010 through fall 2012. No preconstruction installation data were collected for subtidal 2 reefs. Note different axis scales for CPUE by gear type.

Table 4. Mean catch per unit effort (standard error) for gill net (per hour) at reference and reef sites at Vermilion Cove, Louisiana. "Total" indicates the overall number of individuals. All data are postconstruction as indicated in table 1. Data represent uneven efforts and years across treatments (subtidal and intertidal: 9 sample events X 2 replicates X 2 gill net sets = 36 gill net samples collected in 2011 and 2012; intertidal gap: 8 sample events X 2 replicates X 2 gill net sets = 32 gill net samples collected in 2011 and 2012; subtidal 2 = 2 events X 2 replicates X 2 gill nets = 8 gill net samples collected in 2012).

Species	Common name	Total	Reference	Subtidal	Subtidal 2	Intertidal	Intertidal Gap
Carcharhinus leucas	Bull shark	38	1.7 (0.3)	2.3 (0.5)	1.0 (0.0)	2.8 (0.8)	1.3 (0.3)
Ariopsis felis	Hardhead catfish	33	1.6 (0.4)	1.4 (0.4)	1.0 (0.0)	2.2 (1.0)	2.0 (0.0)
Callinectes sapidus	Blue crab	8	1.0 (0.0)	1.0 (0.0)	0 (0.0)	1.7 (0.7)	1.0 (0.0)
Micropogonias undulates	Atlantic croaker	8	0 (0.0)	1.0 (0.0)	2.0 (0.0)	1.0 (0.0)	1.0 (0.0)
Pogonias cromis	Black drum	7	1.0 (0.0)	1.0 (0.0)	0 (0.0)	1.5 (0.5)	1.0 (0.0)
Paralichthys lethostigma	Southern flounder	7	0 (0.0)	0 (0.0)	0 (0.0)	6.0 (0.0)	1.0 (0.0)
Dorosoma cepedianum	Gizzard shad	6	0 (0.0)	1.0 (0.0)	0 (0.0)	1.0 (0.0)	1.0 (0.0)
Brevoortia patronus	Gulf menhaden	5	2.0 (0.0)	0 (0.0)	0 (0.0)	1.5 (0.5)	0 (0.0)
Sciaenops ocellatus	Red drum	4	1.0 (0.0)	0 (0.0)	0 (0.0)	1.0 (0.0)	1.0 (0.0)
Cynoscion nebulosus	Spotted seatrout	4	0 (0.0)	1.0 (0.0)	0 (0.0)	1.5 (0.5)	0 (0.0)
Mugil cephalus	Striped mullet	3	0 (0.0)	0 (0.0)	0 (0.0)	3.0 (0.0)	0 (0.0)
Bagre marinus	Gafftopsail catfish	2	1.0 (0.0)	0 (0.0)	0 (0.0)	1.0 (0.0)	0 (0.0)
Alosa chrysochloris	Skipjack herring	1	0 (0.0)	0 (0.0)	0 (0.0)	1.0 (0.0)	0 (0.0)
Archosargus probatocephalus	Sheepshead	1	0 (0.0)	0 (0.0)	0 (0.0)	0 (0.0)	1.0 (0.0)
Bairdiella chrysoura	Silver perch	1	0 (0.0)	0 (0.0)	0 (0.0)	1.0 (0.0)	0 (0.0)
Dasyatis americana	Southern stingray	1	0 (0.0)	1.0 (0.0)	0 (0.0)	0 (0.0)	0 (0.0)
Atractosteus spatula	Alligator gar	1	0 (0.0)	1.0 (0.0)	0 (0.0)	0 (0.0)	0 (0.0)
Dorosoma petenense	Threadfin shad	1	0 (0.0)	1.0 (0.0)	0 (0.0)	0 (0.0)	0 (0.0)
Total		131	2.4 (0.6)	2.2 (0.6)	2.0 (1.0)	4.5 (1.7)	2.0 (0.6)

28

A total of 113 seine samples were collected over eight sampling periods. In total, 6,263 individuals, consisting of 33 species of fish and invertebrates were collected by using the seine. CPUE ranged from 33.3 ± 24.6 to 62.9 ± 21.6, whereas species richness ranged from 2.0 ± 0.7 to 5.6 ± 0.7 (fig. 11). For postconstruction data, 28 species (5,563 individuals) were collected across reference and reef sites (table 5). The most abundant organisms postconstruction were bay anchovy (*Anchoa mitchilli*), grass shrimp (*Palaeomonetes pugio*), and white shrimp (*Litopenaeus setiferus*), accounting for 89.2 percent of the postconstruction catch by abundance.

Table 5. Mean catch per unit effort (standard error) for seine (per 10-meter seine) at reference and reef sites at Vermilion Cove, Louisiana. "Total" indicates the overall number of individuals. All data are postconstruction as indicated in tables 1 and 3. Data represent uneven efforts and years across treatments (subtidal and intertidal: 9 sample events X 2 replicates X 2 seine pulls = 36 seine samples collected in 2011 and 2012; intertidal gap: 8 sample events X 2 replicates X 2 seine pulls = 32 seine samples collected in 2011 and 2012; subtidal 2 = 2 events x 2 replicates x 2 seine pulls = 8 seine samples collected in 2012).

Species	Common name	Total	Reference	Subtidal	Subtidal 2	Intertidal	Intertidal Gap
Anchoa mitchilli	Bay anchovy	4,182	60.7 (18.1)	52.9 (13.9)	57.0 (47.0)	50.3 (25.2)	61.5 (18.2)
Palaemonetes pugio	Grass shrimp	465	7.7 (2.2)	7.8 (2.3)	1.0 (0.0)	15.3 (6.2)	5.1 (1.4)
Litopenaeus setiferus	White shrimp	316	6.0 (2.1)	8.7 (3.7)	7.0 (0.0)	7.8 (2.8)	3.9 (0.6)
Mugil cephalus	Striped mullet	153	1.2 (0.2)	3.9 (2.3)	0 (0.0)	21.3 (14.3)	6.2 (2.5)
Brevoortia patronus	Gulf menhaden	143	5.0 (1.0)	4.4 (2.3)	0 (0.0)	9.8 (2.8)	2.0 (0.0)
Membras martinica	Rough silverside	143	3.0 (0.0)	37.0 (10.0)	2.0 (0.0)	9.7 (8.7)	8.8 (6.4)
Farfantepenaeus aztecus	Brown shrimp	29	0 (0.0)	2.5 (1.0)	0 (0.0)	1.6 (0.4)	1.5 (0.3)
Callinectes sapidus	Blue crab	26	1.0 (0.0)	1.0 (0.0)	0 (0.0)	1.6 (0.4)	1.0 (0.0)
Bairdiella chrysoura	Silver perch	24	0 (0.0)	2.2 (0.7)	0 (0.0)	1.7 (0.7)	2.0 (0.4)
Cynoscion arenarius	Sandtrout	23	1.0 (0.0)	3.0 (1.4)	1.0 (0.0)	1.7 (0.7)	1.3 (0.3)
Oligoplites saurus	Leatherjack	18	1.0 (0.0)	1.5 (0.5)	1.0 (0.0)	1.3 (0.3)	1.3 (0.3)
Micropogonias undulatus	Atlantic croaker	9	2.0 (0.0)	2.0 (0.0)	0 (0.0)	1.3 (0.3)	0 (0.0)
Elops saurus	Ladyfish	7	2.0 (0.6)	1.0 (0.0)	0 (0.0)	0 (0.0)	0 (0.0)
Anchoa hepsetus	Striped anchovy	4	1.0 (0.0)	2.0 (0.0)	0 (0.0)	0 (0.0)	0 (0.0)
Menida beryllina	Inland silverside	3	0 (0.0)	1.0 (0.0)	0 (0.0)	1.0 (0.0)	1.0 (0.0)
Dorosoma cepedianum	Gizzard shad	3	0 (0.0)	3.0 (0.0)	0 (0.0)	0 (0.0)	0 (0.0)
Gobionellus boleosoma	Darter goby	3	0 (0.0)	2.0 (0.0)	0 (0.0)	1.0 (0.0)	0 (0.0)
Bagre marinus	Gaftopsail catfish	2	0 (0.0)	1.0 (0.0)	0 (0.0)	1.0 (0.0)	0 (0.0)
Alosa chrysochloris	Skipjack herring	1	1.0 (0.0)	0 (0.0)	0 (0.0)	0 (0.0)	0 (0.0)
Fundulus jenkinsi	Saltmarsh minnow	1	0 (0.0)	1.0 (0.0)	0 (0.0)	0 (0.0)	0 (0.0)
Fundulus grandis	Gulf killifish	1	0 (0.0)	0 (0.0)	0 (0.0)	1.0 (0.0)	0 (0.0)
Gobiosoma bosc	Naked goby	1	1.0 (0.0)	0 (0.0)	0 (0.0)	0 (0.0)	0 (0.0)
Lagodon rhomboides	Pinfish	1	1.0 (0.0)	0 (0.0)	0 (0.0)	0 (0.0)	0 (0.0)
Dorosoma petenense	Threadfin shad	1	0 (0.0)	0 (0.0)	0 (0.0)	0 (0.0)	1.0 (0.0)
Caranx sp.	unk. Jack	1	0 (0.0)	1.0 (0.0)	0 (0.0)	0 (0.0)	0 (0.0)
Paralichthys lethostigma	Southern flounder	1	0 (0.0)	0 (0.0)	0 (0.0)	1.0 (0.0)	0 (0.0)
Strongylura marina	Atlantic needlefish	1	0 (0.0)	1.0 (0.0)	0 (0.0)	0 (0.0)	0 (0.0)
Micropanope sculptipes	Sculpted mud crab	1	1.0 (0.0)	0 (0.0)	0 (0.0)	0 (0.0)	0 (0.0)
Total		5,563	46.8 (13.4)	59.2 (13.8)	33.3 (24.6)	62.9 (21.6)	62.1 (16.6)

A total of 330 cast net samples were collected over 9 sampling periods. In total, 2,167 individuals, consisting of 29 species of fish and invertebrates were collected. CPUE ranged from 2.8 ± 0.7 to 12.9 ± 7.7, whereas species richness ranged from 0.8 ± 0.3 to 2.1 ± 0.2 (fig. 11). Of the postconstruction data, 1,760 individuals consisting of 25 species were collected (table 6). The most abundant organisms were Gulf menhaden (*Brevoortia patronus*), bay anchovy, and white shrimp, accounting for 73.4 percent of the postconstruction catch by abundance.

Table 6. Mean catch per unit effort (standard error) for cast net throw at reference and reef sites at Vermilion Cove, Louisiana. "Total" indicates the overall number of individuals. All data are postconstruction as indicated in table 1. Data represent uneven efforts and years across treatments (subtidal and intertidal: 9 sample events X 2 replicates X 5 cast net throws = 90 cast net samples collected in 2011 and 2012; intertidal gap: 8 sample events X 2 replicates X 5 cast net throws = 80 cast net samples collected in 2011 and 2012; subtidal 2 = 2 events X 2 replicates X 5 cast net throws = 20 cast net samples collected in 2012).

Species	Common name	Total	Reference	Subtidal	Subtidal 2	Intertidal	Intertidal Gap
Brevoortia patronus	Gulf menhaden	940	2.7 (0.7)	7.5 (2.7)	15.0 (0.0)	67.6 (45.4)	4.0 (2.0)
Anchoa mitchilli	Bay anchovy	219	2.4 (0.5)	3.6 (1.0)	7.0 (6.0)	1.9 (0.5)	4.0 (1.6)
Litopenaeus setiferus	White shrimp	132	2.8 (0.7)	2.6 (0.4)	1.0 (0.0)	2.1 (0.4)	2.0 (0.7)
Mugil cephalus	Striped mullet	116	2.0 (0.8)	1.4 (0.2)	1.0 (0.0)	3.5 (0.9)	8.5 (3.8)
Membras martinica	Rough silverside	114	4.0 (1.5)	4.2 (1.4)	8.0 (7.0)	2.3 (1.0)	2.0 (0.6)
Palaemonetes pugio	Grass shrimp	94	4.4 (1.7)	3.2 (0.9)	0 (0.0)	2.0 (1.0)	0 (0.0)
Farfantepenaeus aztecus	Brown shrimp	85	1.1 (0.1)	1.0 (0.0)	0 (0.0)	1.2 (0.2)	1.5 (0.5)
Micropogonias undulatus	Atlantic croaker	15	1.5 (0.5)	1.2 (0.2)	1.0 (0.0)	1.0 (0.0)	1.0 (0.0)
Cynoscion arenarius	Sandtrout	11	1.0 (0.0)	1.3 (0.3)	0 (0.0)	1.0 (0.0)	1.0 (0.0)
Ariopsis felis	Hardhead catfish	5	0 (0.0)	1.0 (0.0)	0 (0.0)	1.0 (0.0)	0 (0.0)
Menidia beryllina	Inland silverside	4	0 (0.0)	2.0 (0.0)	0 (0.0)	2.0 (0.0)	0 (0.0)
Bagre marinus	Gaftopsail catfish	3	0 (0.0)	0 (0.0)	0 (0.0)	1.0 (0.0)	0 (0.0)
Bairdiella chrysoura	Silver perch	3	1.0 (0.0)	1.0 (0.0)	0 (0.0)	0 (0.0)	0 (0.0)
Dorosoma cepedianum	Gizzard shad	3	0 (0.0)	3.0 (0.0)	0 (0.0)	0 (0.0)	0 (0.0)
Scianidae	unk. croaker/drum	2	1.0 (0.0)	1.0 (0.0)	0 (0.0)	0 (0.0)	0 (0.0)
Callinectes sapidus	Blue crab	2	1.0 (0.0)	0 (0.0)	0 (0.0)	0 (0.0)	0 (0.0)
Lagodon rhomboides	Pinfish	2	1.0 (0.0)	0 (0.0)	1.0 (0.0)	0 (0.0)	0 (0.0)
Leiostomus xanthurus	Spot	2	0 (0.0)	0 (0.0)	0 (0.0)	1.0 (0.0)	1.0 (0.0)
Anchoa hepsetus	Striped anchovy	2	2.0 (0.0)	0 (0.0)	0 (0.0)	0 (0.0)	0 (0.0)
Eurypanopeus depressus	Depressed mud crab	1	0 (0.0)	1.0 (0.0)	0 (0.0)	0 (0.0)	0 (0.0)
Strongylura marina	Atlantic needlefish	1	0 (0.0)	0 (0.0)	1.0 (0.0)	0 (0.0)	0 (0.0)
Cynoscion nebulosus	Spotted seatrout	1	0 (0.0)	0 (0.0)	0 (0.0)	1.0 (0.0)	0 (0.0)
Paralichthys lethostigma	Southern flounder	1	0 (0.0)	1.0 (0.0)	0 (0.0)	0 (0.0)	0 (0.0)
Oligoplites saurus	Leatherjack	1	0 (0.0)	1.0 (0.0)	0 (0.0)	0 (0.0)	0 (0.0)
Cynoscion nothus	Silver seatrout	1	0 (0.0)	1.0 (0.0)	0 (0.0)	0 (0.0)	0 (0.0)
Total		1,760	3.3 (0.6)	4.1 (0.7)	6.9 (4.1)	12.9 (7.7)	2.8 (0.7)

A total of 48 substrate trays were deployed in Vermilion Cove during 2011 and 2012; however, only 41 were recovered and counted. In total, 2,928 individuals were identified (table 7). The most abundant organisms overall were grass shrimp (*P. pugio*), Harris mud crab (*Rhithropanopeus harrisii*), blue crab (*Callinectes sapidus*), and naked goby (*Gobiosoma bosc*), accounting for 97.1 percent of the total catch. Trays at reference sites had a mean catch of 27.3 ± 12.7 individuals m^{-2}, whereas trays at reef sites had a mean catch of 13.2 ± 2.9 individuals m^{-2}. Seven species were unique to reef trays and included two known reef residents (darter goby, feathered blenny) and several mud crabs which are known to aggregate around reefs.

Table 7. Density (standard error) of species collected on substrate trays deployed near reference, subtidal, intertidal, and intertidal-gap sites at Vermilion Cove, Louisiana. "Total" indicates the overall number of individuals. Trays were deployed for 2-3 weeks in late summer of both 2011 and 2012.

Species	Common name	Total	Mean individuals m^{-2}		
			Overall	Reef	Reference
Palaemonetes pugio	Grass shrimp	1,723	261.1 (54.3)	158.4 (29.7)	774.5 (151.1)
Rhithropanopeus harrisii	Harris mud crab	494	77.4 (24.4)	84.0 (28.1)	36.4 (7.2)
Callinectes sapidus	Blue crab	455	64.6 (7.4)	69.7 (8.4)	37.3 (6.3)
Gobiosoma bosc	Naked goby	171	28.8 (7.7)	32.4 (9.3)	12.7 (3.3)
Gobiosox strumosus	Skilletfish	43	10.3 (2.2)	10.6 (2.4)	4.5 (0.0)
Gobionellus boleosoma	Darter goby	14	9.1 (3.0)	9.1 (3.0)	0.0
Alpheus sp.	Snapping shrimp	6	5.5 (0.9)	5.5 (0.9)	0.0
Eurypanopeus depressus	Depressed mud crab	5	5.7 (1.1)	5.7 (1.1)	0.0
Farfantepenaeus aztecus	Brown shrimp	4	18.2 (0.0)	18.2 (0.0)	0.0
Litopenaeus setiferus	White shrimp	3	6.8 (2.3)	6.8 (2.3)	0.0
Panopeus simpsoni	Oystershell mud crab	3	6.8 (2.3)	6.8 (2.3)	0.0
Hypsoblennius hentzi	Feathered blenny	2	4.5 (0.0)	4.5 0.0)	4.5 (0.0)
Menippe adina	Gulf stone crab	2	9.1 (0.0)	9.1 (0.0)	0.0
Myrophis punctatus	Speckled worm-eel	2	4.5 (0.0)	4.5 (0.0)	4.5 (0.0)
Clibanarisu vittatus	Thinstripe hermit crab	1	4.5 (0.0)	4.5 (0.0)	4.5 (0.0)
	Total	2,928	15.8 (3.3)	13.2 (2.9)	27.3 (12.7)

Mean density of species collected in trays was much lower than two recent projects that used the same gear type (Lake Fortuna: 448.3 ± 63.8 individuals m^{-2}; Grand Isle: 332.9 ± 35.4 individuals m^{-2}; La Peyre, unpub. data). Vermilion Cove is lower salinity than these sites which may explain some of the difference. Other published information on benthic communities is not as directly comparable because of slight differences in gear use, including the lack of an enclosure net. For example, Plunket and LaPeyre (2005) used open trays to sample harvested oyster leases in Barataria Bay, La., and reported lower densities of fish (13.9 individuals m^{-2}) and invertebrates (168.4 individuals m^{-2}). Other tray studies (Tolley and Volety, 2005), and drop sampling studies (Shervette and Gelwick, 2008; Stunz and others, 2010) on other oyster reefs in the northern Gulf of Mexico also reported densities more similar to those found in the present study.

Southwest Pass

Shoreline Stabilization

Mean shoreline retreat at Southwest Pass sites from August 2011 to July 2012, was 26.7 ± 2.9 cm mo^{-1}. This rate presents retreat for the year preconstruction. These data will provide a baseline measure and marker for continued collection of shoreline movement data at these sites.

Mean soil percentage of organic matter was 11.8 ± 0.4 percent across all sample dates and sites (preconstruction and postconstruction combined). Mean percentage of vegetative cover across all sample dates and treatments at Southwest Pass was 31.3 ± 4.2 percent. The most abundant species were inland saltgrass (*Distichlis spicata*) and *Juncus roemerianus*. Other species present included *Scirpus robusta, Spartina alterniflora, Phragmites australis, Borrichia frutescens,* and *Batis maritima*. Mean live aboveground vegetative biomass was 584.6 ± 8.7 g m^{-2} (fig. 12). There were no significant differences between treatment or sample date for soil percent organic matter, percent vegetative cover, or aboveground biomass. Mean belowground vegetative biomass differed between preconstruction and postconstruction samples with higher biomass preconstruction (304.3 ± 57.3 g m^{-2}) as compared to postconstruction (160.2 ± 18.8 g m^{-2}) (p=0.007). Postconstruction samples were taken shortly after completion of construction (fig. 12).

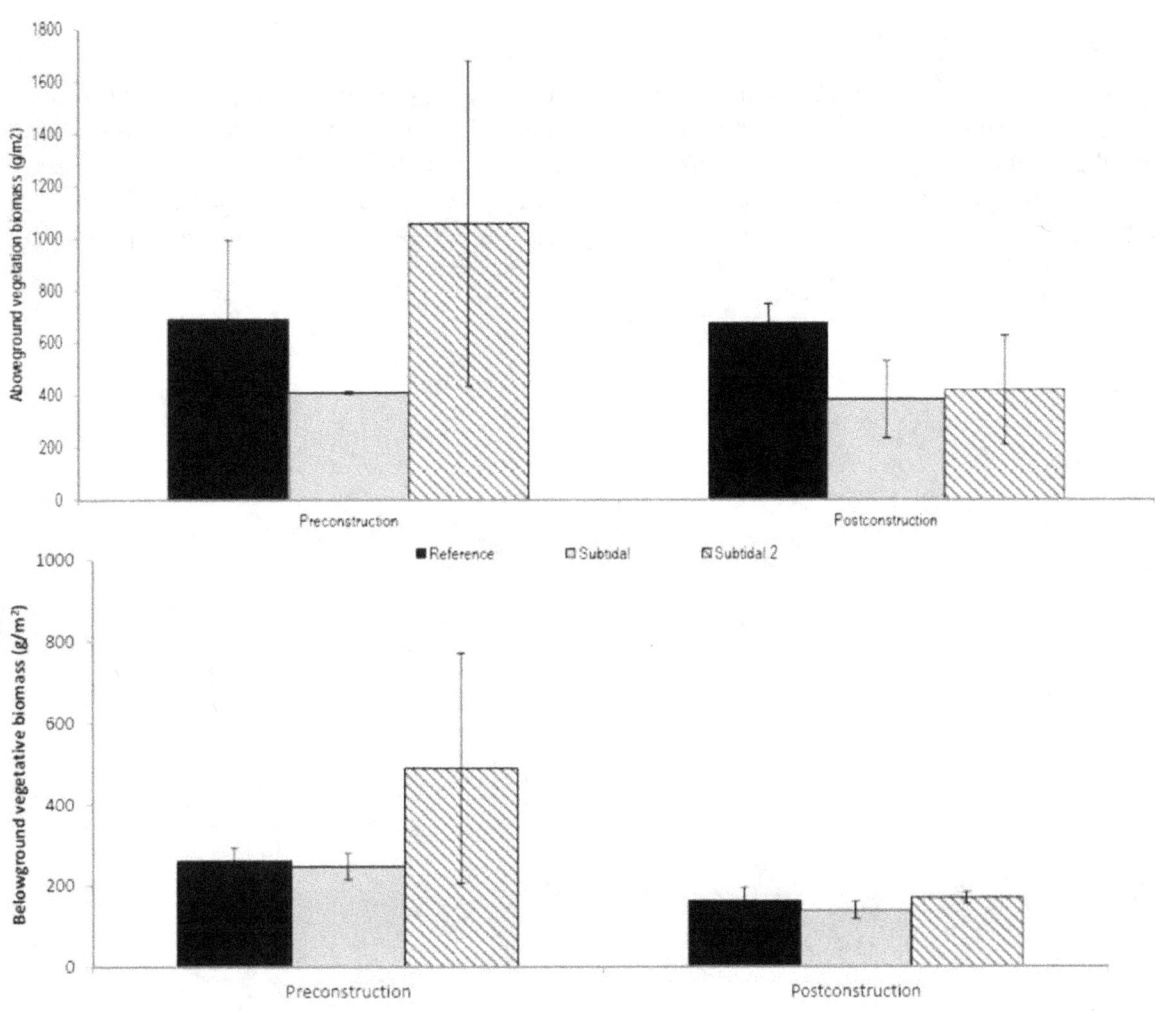

Figure 12.   Mean aboveground and belowground vegetative biomass (grams per square meter [g m^{-2}]) of reference and treatments at Southwest Pass, Louisiana, sites. Bars represent standard error. Preconstruction samples were collected in August 2011; postconstruction samples were collected in July 2012 after the June 2012 construction.

Reef Sustainability

Because of construction ending in June 2012, there was insufficient time to allow for recruitment (attachment plus survival) on the reefs. Further sampling over a longer time period would be necessary to determine if these sites are conducive to oyster recruitment and growth.

Environmental Variables

Water quality parameters are reported as ranges across all dates and treatment types (table 3). Because only summer samples were collected for this study area, ranges reported do not likely reflect the range occurring throughout the year. No differences by site were expected or recorded. Daily mean water levels from the continuous data recorder at a nearby CRMS sites (CRMS 0541) show that subtidal 2 reefs are exposed for 2 percent of the time, and subtidal reefs are exposed for less than 1 percent of the time (fig. 13).

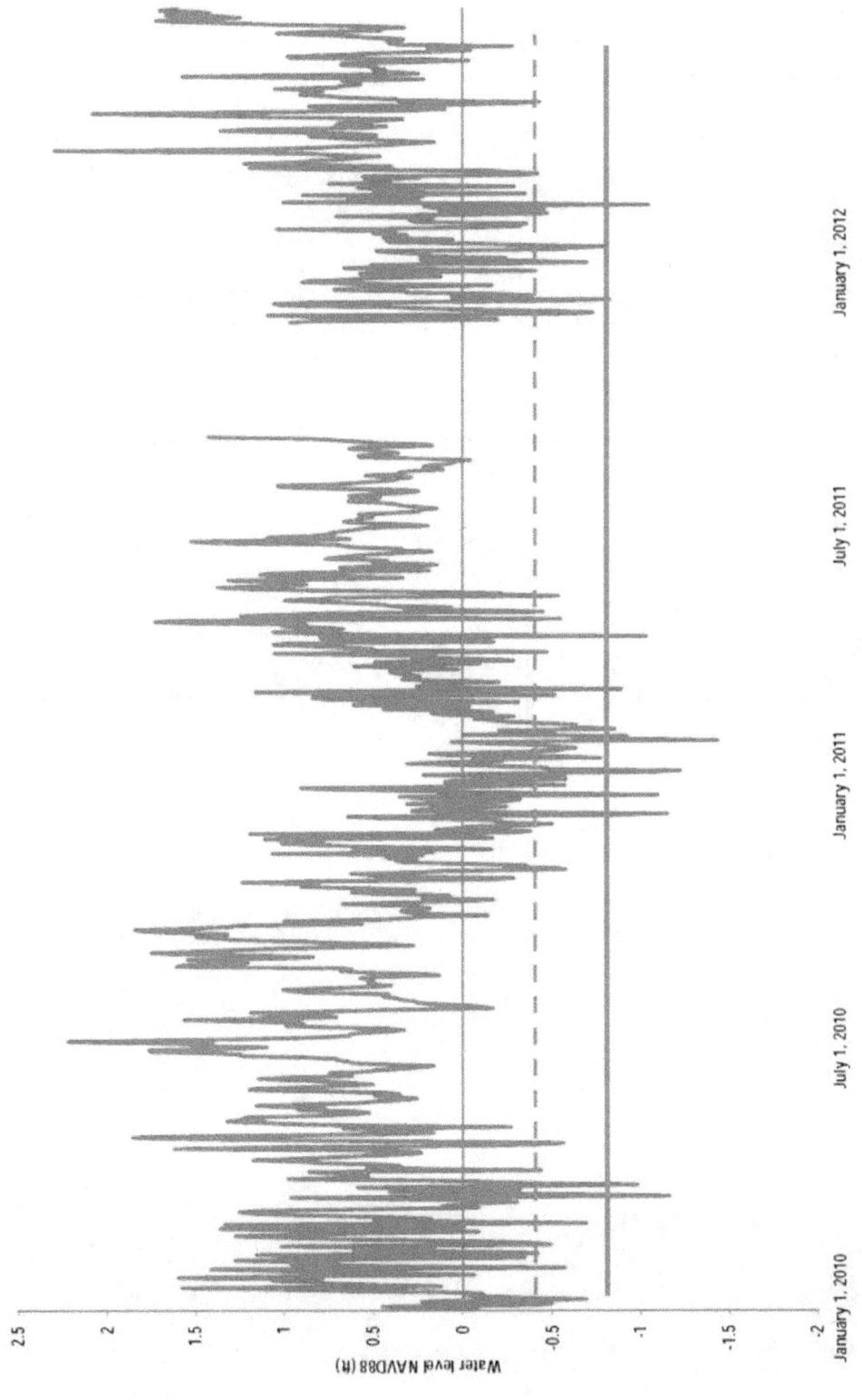

The dashed grey line represents the elevation of the subtidal 2 reefs (2 percent of the time the reef top is above water); the solid grey line is the subtidal reef (less than 1 percent of the time the reef top is above water).

Figure 13.   Daily mean water levels at Southwest Pass, Louisiana (CRMS0541; LOCPR, 2012), from January 2010 to June 2012. Data are referenced to NAVD 88 (feet).

Habitat Enhancement

No preconstruction nekton data were collected at Southwest Pass. A total of 12 gill net samples were collected over 2 sampling periods postconstruction (June, July 2012). Overall, 46 individuals from seven species were caught (table 8). Hardhead catfish (*A. felis*) were the most abundant organism, accounting for 76.1 percent of the total catch. There were no statistically significant differences in CPUE or species richness between treatment and reference sites (fig. 14).

Table 8. Mean catch per unit effort for gill net (per hour) at reference and reef sites at Southwest Pass, Louisiana, sites. "Total" indicates the overall number of individuals. All data are postconstruction as indicated in table 2. Data represent two summer 2012 sample events (2 events X 2 replicates X 2 gill net sets = 8 sets per treatment).

Species	Common name	Total	Reference	Subtidal	Subtidal 2
Ariopsis felis	Hardhead catfish	35	4.3 (0.9)	3.3 (1.9)	4.0 (1.2)
Carcharhinus leucas	Bull shark	5	1.0 (0.0)	1.0 (0.0)	1.5 (0.5)
Bagre marinus	Gaftopsail catfish	2	1.0 (0.0)	0 (0.0)	1.0 (0.0)
Callinectes sapidus	Blue crab	1	0 (0.0)	1.0 (0.0)	0 (0.0)
Micropogonias undulates	Atlantic croaker	1	0 (0.0)	1.0 (0.0)	0 (0.0)
Cynoscion nebulosus	Spotted seatrout	1	0 (0.0)	0 (0.0)	1.0 (0.0)
Peprilus alepidotus	Harvestfish	1	1.0 (0.0)	0 (0.0)	0 (0.0)
	Total	46	4.0 (1.4)	3.3 (1.7)	4.3 (1.5)

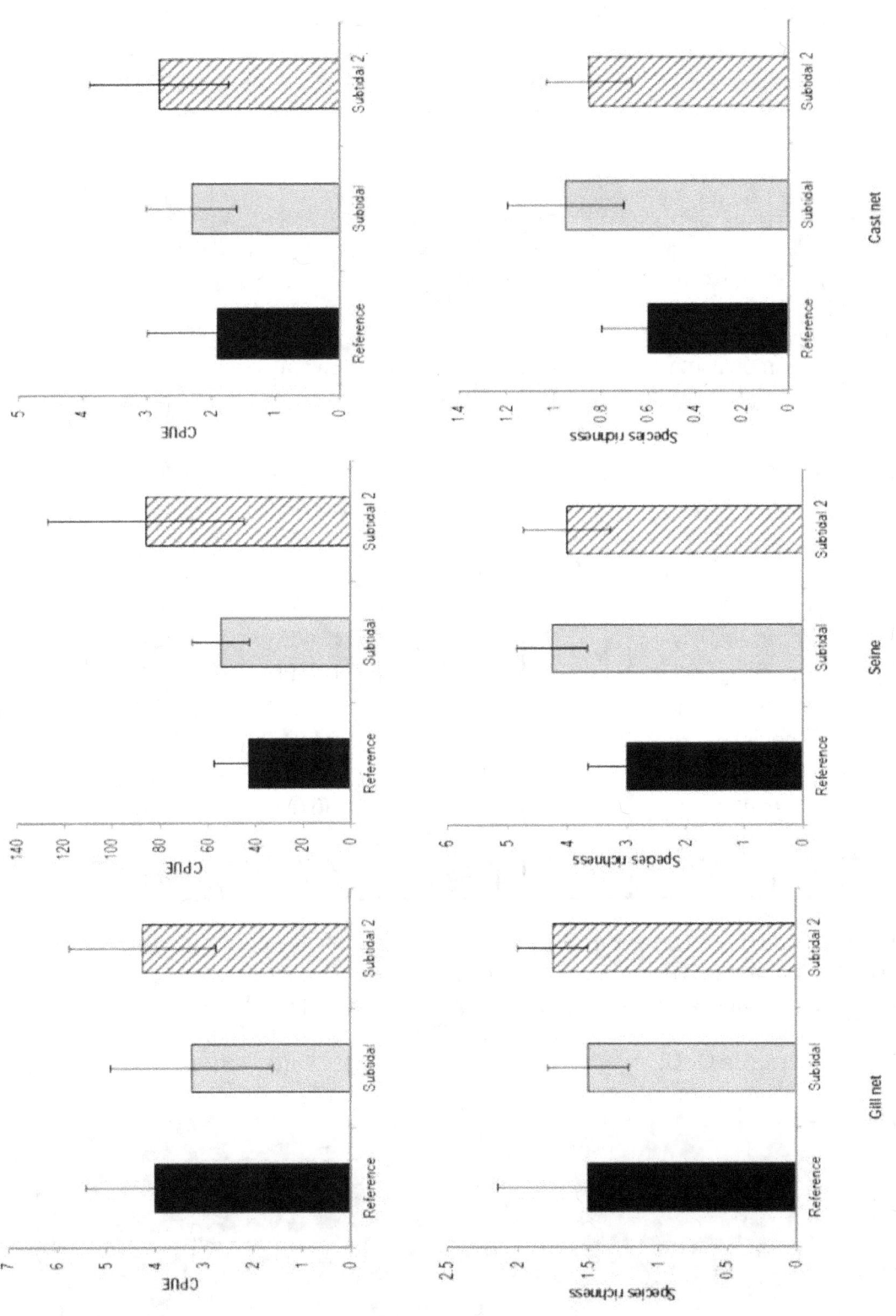

Figure 14. Mean catch per unit effort (CPUE) and number of species caught with gill nets, seines, and cast-nets at reference, subtidal, and subtidal 2 sites at Southwest Pass, Louisiana. Bars represent standard error. All data are postconstruction. Note different axes scales for CPUE.

Overall, 24 seine samples were collected over two sample dates postconstruction at Southwest Pass. In total, 1,462 individuals consisting of 14 species were caught (table 9). The most abundant species was bay anchovy (*A. michilli*), which accounted for 83.7 percent of the overall catch. Other dominant species included white shrimp (*L. setiferus*) and Gulf menhaden (*B. patronus*).There were no statistically significant differences in CPUE or number of species caught between treatments (fig. 14).

Table 9. Mean catch per unit for seine (10-meter seine) at reference and reef sites at Southwest Pass, Louisiana. "Total" indicates the overall number of individuals. All data are postconstruction as indicated in tables 2 and 3. Data represent two summer 2012 sample events (2 events X 2 replicates X 2 seine pulls = 8 seine pulls per treatment).

Species	Common name	Total	Reference	Subtidal	Subtidal 2
Anchoa mitchilli	Bay anchovy	1,224	43.7 (15.7)	41.3 (12.1)	73.5 (41.9)
Litopenaeus setiferus	White shrimp	76	3.8 (1.7)	4.3 (1.1)	15.5 (0.5)
Brevoortia patronus	Gulf menhaden	53	1.0 (0.0)	18.5 (16.5)	7.5 (6.5)
Farfantepenaeus aztecus	Brown shrimp	39	1.7 (0.7)	2.5 (0.7)	3.8 (1.0)
Palaemonetes pugio	Grass shrimp	34	2.5 (0.5)	3.0 (1.2)	3.4 (1.0)
Micropogonias undulatus	Atlantic croaker	8	2.0 (0.0)	2.0 (1.0)	1.0 (0.0)
Bairdiella chrysoura	Silver perch	7	0 (0.0)	1.0 (0.0)	1.7 (0.7)
Anchoa hepsetus	Striped anchovy	6	1.0 (0.0)	4.0 (0.0)	1.0 (0.0)
Callinectes sapidus	Blue crab	5	1.0 (0.0)	1.0 (0.0)	2.0 (0.0)
Membras martinica	Rough silverside	4	0 (0.0)	0 (0.0)	2.0 (1.0)
Cynoscion arenarius	Sandtrout	2	1.0 (0.0)	1.0 (0.0)	0 (0.0)
Cynoscion nebulosus	Spotted seatrout	2	2.0 (0.0)	0 (0.0)	0 (0.0)
Gobiosoma bosc	Naked goby	1	0 (0.0)	0 (0.0)	1.0 (0.0)
Synodus foetens	Inshore lizzardfish	1	1.0 (0.0)	0 (0.0)	0 (0.0)
	Total	1,462	42.6 (14.7)	54.5 (12.0)	85.6 (41.0)

A total of 60 cast net samples, collected over 2 sampling periods postconstruction, were collected at Southwest Pass, Louisiana. Overall, 140 individuals consisting of 12 species were caught (table 10). The most abundant species were bay anchovy (*A. mitchilli*) and brown shrimp (*Farfantepenaeus aztecus*), which accounted for 76.4 percent of the overall catch. There were no statistically significant differences in CPUE or species richness between treatments (fig. 14).

Table 10. Mean catch per unit effort for cast net throws at reference and reef sites at Southwest Pass, Louisiana. "Total" indicates the overall number of individuals. All data are postconstruction as indicated in tables 2 and 3. Data represent two summer 2012 sample events (2 events X 2 replicates X 5 cast net throws = 20 cast net throws per treatment).

Species	Common name	Total	Reference	Subtidal	Subtidal 2
Anchoa mitchilli	Bay anchovy	93	9.0 (5.1)	4.4 (1.2)	5.8 (2.6)
Farfantepenaeus aztecus	Brown shrimp	14	1.5 (0.3)	1.0 (0.0)	1.0 (0.0)
Brevoortia patronus	Gulf menhaden	11	0 (0.0)	0 (0.0)	11.0 (0.0)
Membras martinica	Rough silverside	7	1.0 (0.0)	2.0 (0.0)	1.0 (0.0)
Micropogonias undulates	Atlantic croaker	5	0 (0.0)	1.3 (0.3)	1.0 (0.0)
Ariopsis felis	Hardhead catfish	3	0 (0.0)	1.0 (0.0)	1.0 (0.0)
Trachinotus carolinus	Pompano	2	1.0 (0.0)	1.0 (0.0)	0 (0.0)
Palaemonetes pugio	Grass shrimp	1	0 (0.0)	0 (0.0)	1.0 (0.0)
Mugil cephalus	Striped mullet	1	1.0 (0.0)	0 (0.0)	0 (0.0)
Callinectes sapidus	Blue crab	1	0 (0.0)	0 (0.0)	1.0 (0.0)
Bairdiella chrysoura	Silver perch	1	1.0 (0.0)	0 (0.0)	0 (0.0)
Strongylura marina	Atlantic needlefish	1	1.0 (0.0)	0 (0.0)	0 (0.0)
	Total	140	1.9 (1.1)	2.3 (0.7)	2.8 (1.1)

Summary and Conclusions

Because the original project called for comparison of subtidal and intertidal reef development and performance, the range of reef "ages" (from 1 to 30 months [mo]), combined with continued construction activities in the vicinity of the project, make any interpretation of the data, or reef development trajectories difficult at this stage. This project did successfully collect extensive detailed data on shoreline position and movement, on-reef oyster recruitment and survival, adjacent marsh vigor, and nekton communities by using the experimental reef areas from 2010 to 2012, thus providing a valuable baseline of data for future evaluations.

Through 2010 and 2011 there was no development of a surviving oyster reef community on reefs at Vermilion Cove. As of July 2012, oysters recruited in fall 2011 were thriving, suggesting that perhaps this last year provided conditions for the development of a small reef community; however, it is difficult to interpret much from these data. During 2010 and 2011, confounding factors of continued construction activities very near established reefs, unidentified potential impacts of the Deepwater Horizon oil spill (2010), or low water impacts from the 100-year floods in 2011 all may have contributed to our lack of viable oyster recruitment. Alternatively, because this area chosen for the creation of the reefs is well known to regularly experience low salinity caused by influence of the Atchafalaya River, and subsequently low growth and survival of oysters such that most oyster leases in the area are only productive approximately every 10 years, it is equally likely that the provision of the reef substrate must be timed with a successful year for oyster recruitment and survival before the reefs will become established.

Reefs created at Southwest Pass have only been constructed within the last 6 mo of the study, and no recruitment has been noted on the reefs. Southwest Pass is located along a busy navigation channel and is an area with rapid water movement and a relatively steep incline. The sediments in this area are more clay, and there is little shell and hard bottom as is found in Vermilion Cove.

Although recruitment is occurring on the Vermilion Cove reefs, the local environment is not conducive every year to survival and development of the reef; given more years of monitoring, it is quite possible that over time, as appears to happen on the adjacent public seed grounds, conditions may occur which will support good recruitment, survival, and growth of an oyster set. This reef project highlights the need to examine these reef creation projects over the long term to truly identify sustainable reef trajectories; with highly variable salinity regimes in many areas of coastal Louisiana, success or failure may not be determined within a short time frame. For restoration in which immediate reef development is needed, an area known to have only an occasional "good" year for recruitment may not be most conducive to such restoration. Similarly, it is not clear with our current knowledge of oyster biology if Southwest Pass water conditions are conducive to spat recruitment and survival. Further investigation into hydrodynamics of the area and water velocity limits for spat and oysters would provide needed insight.

Because many of the processes identified for monitoring reflect long-term processes, and we were interested initially in comparing the development trajectories of subtidal versus intertidal reefs, future work would be extremely interesting in understanding (1) if there are differences in the development of thriving oyster communities between subtidal and intertidal reefs, based on food availability, exposure and potential predation risks; (2) if subtidal reefs which develop a thriving oyster population will build upwards to resemble the intertidal reefs over time or will develop differently; (3) if subtidal reefs become intertidal reefs, will they then act on shoreline movement in the same way as the artificial intertidal reefs; (4) at what point, or what density and size of oysters, would a measurable water quality effect exist; and (5) do subtidal and intertidal reefs provide different nekton enhancement as measured by community composition, species richness, and abundances?

Cited References

Beck, Steve, 2011, The effects of oyster harvest on resident oyster reef communities and reef structure in coastal Louisiana: Baton Rouge, La., Louisiana State University, M.S. thesis, 134 p.

Coen, L.D., Luckenbach, M.W., and Breitburg, D.L., 1999, The role of oyster reefs as essential fish habitat—A review of current knowledge and some new perspectives, *in* Benaka, L.R., (ed.), Fish habitat—Essential fish habitat and restoration: American Fisheries Society Symposium v. 22, p. 438–454.

Coen, L.D., Brumbaugh, R.D., Bushek, D., Grizzle, R., Luckenbach, M.W., Posey, M.H., Powers, S.P., and Tolley, S.G., 2007, Ecosystem services related to oyster restoration: Marine Ecology Progress Series, v. 341, p. 304–307.

Craft, G, Reader, J., Sacco, J.N., and Broome, S.W., 1999, Twenty-five years of ecosystem development of constructed *Spartina alterniflora* (Loisel) marshes: Ecological Applications, v. 9, p. 1405–1419.

La Peyre, M.K., Gossman, B., Piazza, B., 2008, Short and long-term response of deteriorating brackish marshes and open water ponds to sediment enhancement by thin layer dredge disposal: Estuaries and Coasts, v. 32, p. 390–402.

Lehnert, R.L., and Allen, D.M., 2002, Nekton use of subtidal oyster shell habitat in a southeastern U.S. estuary: Estuaries, v. 25, p. 1015–1024.

LOCPR (Louisiana Office of Coastal Protection and Restoration), 2012, Coastwide Reference Monitoring System-Wetlands Monitoring Data: Strategic Online Natural Resource Information System (SONRIS), accessed December 12, 2012, at http://coastal.louisiana.gov/index.cfm?md=pagebuilder&tmp=home&pid=92.

Meyer, D.L., Townsend, E.C., and Thayer, G.W., 1997, Stabilization and erosion control value of oyster cultch for intertidal marsh: Restoration Ecology, v. 5, p. 93–99.

Odum, E.P., 1969, The strategy of ecosystem development: Science, v. 164, p. 262–270.

Peterson, C.H., Grabowski, J.H., and Powers, S.P., 2003, Estimated enhancement of fish production resulting from restoring oyster reef habitat—Quantitative valuation: Marine Ecology Progress Series, v. 264, p. 251–266.

Piazza, B.P., Banks, P.D., and La Peyre, M.K., 2005, The potential for created oyster shell reefs as a sustainable shoreline protection strategy in Louisiana: Restoration Ecology, v. 13, p. 499–506.

Plunket, J.T., and Peyre, M.K., 2005, Oyster beds as fish and macroinvertebrate habitat in Barataria Bay, Louisiana: Bulletin of Marine Science, v. 77, p. 155–164.

Scyphers, S.B., Powers, S.P., Heck, K.L., Jr., and Byron, D., 2011, Oyster reefs as natural breakwaters mitigate shoreline loss and facilitate fisheries: PLoS One, v. 4, no. 8, e22396, accessed February 1, 2013, at http://www.plosone.org/article/info%3Adoi%2F10.1371%2Fjournal.pone.0022396.

Shervette, V.R., and Gelwick, F., 2008, Seasonal and spatial variations in fish and macroinvertebrate communities of oyster and adjacent habitats in a Mississippi estuary: Estuaries and Coasts, v. 31, p. 584–596.

Stunz, G.W., Minello, T., and Rozas, L., 2010, Relative value of oyster reef as habitat for estuarine nekton in Galveston Bay, Texas: Marine Ecology Progress Series, v. 406, p. 147–159.

Tolley, G., and Volety, A.K., 2005, The role of oysters in habitat use of oyster reefs by resident fishes and decapod crustaceans: Journal of Shellfish Research, v. 24, p. 1007–1012.

Yeager, L.A., and Layman, C.A., 2011, Energy flow to consumers in a sub-tropical oyster reef food web: Aquatic Ecology, v. 45, no. 2, p. 267–277.

Publishing support provided by
Lafayette Publishing Service Center